Contents

Getting the most from this book

Exam tips

Advice on key points in the text to help you learn and recall content, avoid pitfalls, and polish your exam technique in order to boost your grade.

Knowledge check

Rapid-fire questions throughout the Content Guidance section to check your understanding.

Knowledge check answers

1 Turn to the back of the book for the Knowledge check answers.

Summaries

■ Each core topic is rounded off by a bullet-list summary for quick-check reference of what you need to know.

Exam-style questions

Sample student answers

Practise the questions, then look at the student answers that follow.

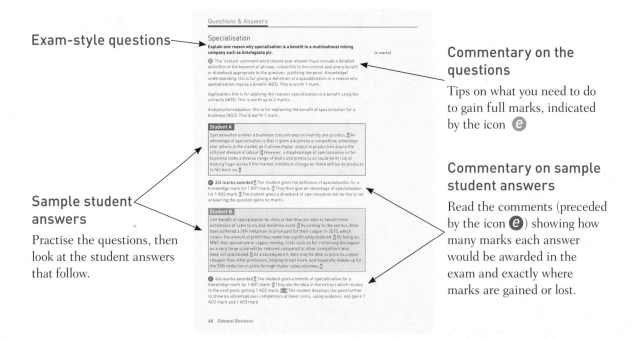

Commentary on the questions

Tips on what you need to do to gain full marks, indicated by the icon **e**

Commentary on sample student answers

Read the comments (preceded by the icon **e**) showing how many marks each answer would be awarded in the exam and exactly where marks are gained or lost.

■ About this book

Student Guide 4, along with its companions Student Guides 1, 2 and 3, has been written with one thing in mind: to provide you with the ideal resource for your revision of Edexcel Business A-level.

In your study of the subject you will look at business in a variety of contexts, small and large, national and global, service and manufacturing.

The themes of A-level Business also include Theme 1: Marketing and people, Theme 2: Managing business activities and Theme 3: Business decisions and strategy. It is very important that you have studied all the themes in order to successfully complete the exams, and you should read Theme 1 in particular as it provides the foundations for this guide.

The focus of Student Guide 4 is as follows:

■ Globalisation – how economies across the world are operating as a large market for a business, what the opportunities and risks are for a business operating globally compared with just in the UK, and the indicators and implications of growth for a business, particularly in Asia, Africa and other developing global markets.

■ International trade and business growth – how a business can grow through exports and imports, the link between business specialisation and competitive advantage, and the link between foreign direct investment and the growth of a business.

■ Factors contributing to increased globalisation – factors that affect a business's ability to trade competitively across different countries, including trade liberalisation, political change, increased investment, migration and structural change in a country.

■ Protectionism and conditions that prompt trade – how trade barriers a country creates can impact on a business's growth and competitive advantage, including tariffs and import quotas and the push and pull factors that can cause a business to trade globally.

■ Assessing a country as a market, production location, including mergers and joint ventures – how a business assesses a global market as a place to compete and/or locate production and the reasons for mergers and joint ventures, including spreading risk, acquiring international brand names and maintaining global competitiveness.

■ Global competitiveness and global marketing – the impact of movements in exchange rates on competitive advantage, global marketing strategy, including the marketing mix, cultural diversity and global niche markets.

■ Cultural and social factors and ethics – the impact of multinational corporations on the local and national economy and the ethics of global trade, including stakeholder conflicts and environmental considerations and how multinational corporations can be controlled.

Content Guidance

The Content Guidance section offers concise coverage combining an overview of key terms and concepts with identification of opportunities for you to illustrate higher-level skills of analysis and evaluation.

Questions & Answers

The Questions & Answers section provides examples of stimulus materials with the various types of questions that you are likely to be faced with: short answer questions, data response and open response questions. The questions give explanations of command words which can be applied to any question with the same word. The answers are also explained in detail, including the grades obtained.

A common problem for students and teachers is the lack of resources and in particular exam-style questions that cover individual areas of study. The questions in this guide are tailored so you can apply your learning while the topic is still fresh in your mind, either during the course or when you have revised a topic in preparation for the examination. Along with the sample answers this should give you a sound basis for sitting your exams in Business.

Pre-existing knowledge

For A-level Business it is recommended that you have already studied Student Guides 1 and 2 before moving on to this guide. This is because a number of the basic business concepts that are discussed in Guide 4 are based on the foundation knowledge of those in the three previous guides. The most important requirement at this stage is an interest in the current news in terms of businesses you are familiar with, such as Apple or McDonald's. Business is a subject that requires you to apply key terms to real businesses so an interest in businesses in the news will help you significantly to contextualise the theories – it is the really enjoyable part of the subject and ultimately allows you to score highly in the exam.

Content Guidance

■ Globalisation

Globalisation is the process by which the world is becoming more and more interconnected as a result of massively increased global trade and cultural exchange. Globalisation has increased the production of goods and services – many businesses no longer trade nationally but now operate internationally as **multinational corporations**, with different parts of the business (known as **subsidiaries**) operating in many countries.

Globalisation has led to a significant increase in trade across world markets and resulted in greater competition.

Growing economies

Growth rate of the UK compared with emerging economies

Growth rate is the rate at which a nation's gross domestic product (GDP) changes/grows from one year to another. **GDP** is the market value of all the goods and services produced in a country in a particular time period. It can be measured in three ways. Output measure is the value of the goods and services produced by all sectors of the economy: agriculture, manufacturing, energy, construction, the service sector and government. Expenditure measure is the value of the goods and services purchased by households and by government, investment in machinery and buildings. It also includes the value of exports minus imports. Income measure is the value of the income generated mostly in terms of profits and wages.

GDP is commonly used to measure the growth of countries and make comparisons.

According to the Office for National Statistics, the UK economy has grown by an average of 2.2% every year since 1956. However, **emerging economies** such as China and India are growing at much faster rates. So some UK businesses boost their growth by focusing on these rapidly emerging economies. Figure 1 shows an example of car production from 2000 to 2015 among the **BRIC economies**, which highlights China's extraordinary economic growth.

> **BRIC economies** The economies of Brazil, Russia, India and China, which are at a similar stage of economic development.

Globalisation The process that has increased the production of goods and services through greater global trade and cultural exchange.

Growth rate The percentage change of a specific variable within a specific time, given a certain context. An economic growth rate is a measure of economic growth from one period to another in percentage terms.

GDP The total value of output in the UK, used to measure change in economic activity.

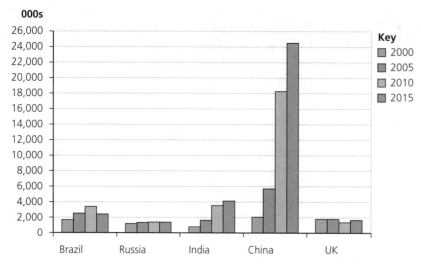

000s

Figure 1 Annual motor vehicle production, BRICs plus UK

Source: OICA 2016

An **emerging economy** describes a nation's economy that is progressing towards becoming more advanced, usually by means of rapid growth and industrialisation. In order to compare the growth rate of the UK with other emerging economies, GDP is often used, which is normally expressed in a common currency such as the US dollar ($). Figure 2 shows current GDP for 20 world economies and the projected GDP by 2030. In 2016 the UK's GDP was the fifth largest in the world, but this is predicted to change by 2030 so that countries such as India, Brazil and Turkey will be bigger.

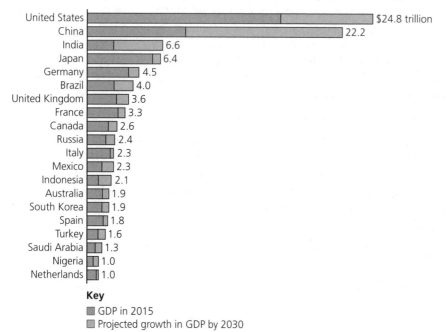

Figure 2 The world's 20 largest economies projected for 2030

Source: US Department of Agriculture

Emerging economy An economy with incomes that are growing but still quite low. Such countries constitute approximately 80% of the global population and represent about 20% of the world's wealth.

Knowledge check 1

a) Give a reason why economies such as the UK have lost out to countries like China in terms of manufacturing.

b) How have economies like the UK responded to the loss of manufacturing?

Comparing GDPs of different countries usually means converting other currencies to the US dollar, which can cause problems as a result of **exchange rates**. Exchange rates vary from month to month for products that are traded between nations (such as cars) but this does not affect products and services that are traded within a country (such as haircuts).

Calculations of GDP based on market exchange rates tend to overestimate the cost of living in poorer developing countries. To try to ensure GDP is measured realistically, a method called **purchasing power parity** (PPP) can be used.

PPP takes a standard shopping basket of goods and prices them for each country. A simple way to explain this is through *The Economist's* Big Mac index, which prices a McDonald's Big Mac using PPP to show the real cost of living. In July 2016, for example, in the UK a Big Mac's PPP price was $3.94 compared with Brazil's price of $4.78.

Growing economic power of countries within Asia, Africa and other parts of the world

Traditionally, western countries such as the UK, Germany and the US have been markets of growth for businesses to target in terms of exports and international trade. However, looking at Figure 2, clearly this is changing rapidly, with developing countries growing much more quickly than western markets due to increased GDP and the corresponding wealth of citizens.

Economies such as China and India have comparatively high levels of investment compared with western countries such as the UK, which brings with it jobs, infrastructure and new markets for businesses to expand into. Other developing countries such as Indonesia and Tanzania have large and growing populations, a good supply of relatively young workers and increased industrialisation of the economy. In July 2016 GDP growth in Indonesia was running at 5.18% compared with 7% in India. Tanzania (in East Africa) has been growing at 7% a year for several years.

Implications of economic growth for individuals and businesses

There are various implications of this economic growth for **businesses**:

- New markets mean expansion and potentially increased profits.
- Products that are mature or even in decline may be given an extension strategy simply by entering a previously untapped market.
- Mergers/takeovers and partnerships can mean a UK business can take advantage of a new market's potential relatively quickly.
- As these may be emerging economies, the workforce tends to have low expectations for pay and conditions, which allows a reduction in unit costs.
- As emerging economies tend to be rich in natural resources, businesses can buy raw materials cheaply, thus reducing unit costs of products.
- Foreign countries are willing to offer incentives such as tax breaks in order to entice multinationals to locate manufacturing in the new market, leading to lower costs.
- Adapting products and services to the local market can increase brand loyalty among new customers and enhance profitability. **Glocalisation** is where a business in a global market customises a product or service to the locality and/or culture so that it is more likely to sell products.

Exchange rate The price of one currency in terms of another.

Purchasing power parity Allows for differences in the cost of living in different countries, which gives more realistic comparisons of GDP.

Glocalisation A combination of the words 'globalisation' and 'localisation', used to describe a product or service that is developed and distributed globally but is also fashioned to accommodate the user or consumer in a local market.

For example, McDonald's strategy is to listen more to local consumers and then act on what they say. The company strives to do this around the world. Some of its local favourites include the McItaly burger in Italy, the Maharaja Mac in India, the McLobster in Canada and the Ebi Filet-O in Japan.

The implications of economic growth for individuals include:

- **lower unemployment** – with higher output and positive economic growth firms tend to employ more workers, creating more employment
- **higher average incomes** – more employment means consumers have greater income, enabling them to enjoy more goods and services and better standards of living
- **improved public services** – with increased tax revenues from businesses the government can spend more on public services, such as healthcare and education
- **investment**, especially **foreign direct investment** (FDI) – economic growth encourages investment and therefore a virtuous cycle of further growth. Foreign businesses can act as the catalyst for growth, which not only benefits individuals through increased standards of living but can also help improve roads and local services.

Indicators of growth

To assess the economic development of a growing economy the following indicators can be used:

- Gross domestic product is the economic activity of a country and shows its ups and downs if measured over time, known as the business cycle.
- GDP per capita is a measure of the total output of a country that takes GDP and divides it by the number of people in the country. The per capita GDP is especially useful when comparing one country's **standard of living** with another, because it shows the countries' relative performance.

Looking at GDP per capita particularly over a period of time and in comparison with that of another economy can be a good indicator of growth. To ensure the comparison is realistic, the PPP figure takes into account that it is cheaper to live in some countries than in others. Table 1 shows both the raw GDP per capita and the adjusted PPP figure for the UK and India. Clearly the UK figures are much greater than India's, which means individuals in the UK have a greater ability to purchase necessities and luxuries from businesses.

The raw figures suggest that UK incomes are 25 times those of Indian incomes; when adjusted for differences in the cost of living (PPP), the difference shrinks to 6.75 times.

Table 1 Incomes in India and the UK: raw data and adjusted to show PPP

	India	UK	Ratio (UK/India)
GDP per capita (2015)	$1,627	$40,933	25 times
GDP per capita at PPP (2015)	$5,730	$38,657	6.75 times

Literacy refers to the percentage of adults who can read and write. According to the OECD's 2016 International Adult Literacy Survey, the differences in average skill levels among OECD countries explain 55% of the differences in economic growth. This

Foreign direct investment The transfer of funds by a foreign business to purchase and acquire physical capital, such as factories and machines.

Exam tip

The examiner often includes charts and graphs about such issues as GDP, so it is particularly important that you are able to interpret the figures and look for trends. You also need to look at the wider measures of the economy discussed in the question in order to be able to evaluate the bigger global market picture.

Standard of living A country's level of wealth, comfort, material goods and necessities available to an average individual.

Knowledge check 2

Give an example of a situation where a UK manufacturer has altered a product for the global market and comment on how successful this has been.

implies that investments in raising the average level of skills could yield large economic returns. According to a report in 2015 by UNESCO, data literacy in 15–24 year olds was 99% in the UK and 89% in India, up from 76% in 2001. Steady increases in the level of literacy may be as important an indicator of economic growth as trends in GDP.

Health is another key factor part-cause and part-effect of economic growth. Key measures include average life expectancy, mortality rates among babies and access to healthcare, all of which are linked to economic growth in an emerging economy. Table 2 gives an example of life expectancy and infant mortality rates.

Table 2 Health statistics: life expectancy and infant mortality rates

	Infant mortality rates (under one year) per 1,000 births, 1960	Infant mortality rates (under one year) per 1,000 births, 2015	Life expectancy (from birth), 1960 (years)	Life expectancy (from birth), 2015 (years)
Ghana	91	43	46	61
Bulgaria	43	9	69	75
Brazil	129	15	54	74
UK	23	4	71	81

Source: World Bank

The **Human Development Index** (HDI) is a weighted mix of indices that shows life expectancy, knowledge (adult literacy and education) and standard of living (GDP per capita). It was launched by the United Nations in 1990 and is measured between 0 and 1. Table 3 shows an example of HDI rankings for different countries – the nearer to 1, the better.

Table 3 HDI ranking and scores, selected countries, 2015

	Rank (out of 180 countries)	HDI score (out of 1.00)
Ghana	140	0.579
Bulgaria	59	0.782
Brazil	75	0.755
UK	14	0.909

Source: World Bank

The problems with using indices as economic growth measurements include the fact that they all consider the average of the population without taking into account that there may be large imbalances in the country and that in certain countries the actual data are not always reliable.

International trade and business growth

International trade is the exchange of capital, goods and services across international borders or territories. Reasons businesses undertake international trade include accessing new markets for growth and profit, increased efficiency of production, reductions in cost and increases in quality. Businesses will be looking to use any advantage they have over their rivals in the supply of goods or services.

Business growth can be achieved through international trade and measured in a number of ways, including assets, sales revenue, operating profit and market share. Growth may provide a multinational business with advantages such as greater sales volume, higher market share, economies of scale and larger profits.

Knowledge check 3

Give one reason why education is such an important factor in the growth of emerging economies.

Exam tip

Remember that a lot of the indicators discussed are general. You need to look at the specific evidence you are presented with and your wider knowledge of global business to identify positive and negative impacts on international businesses. Evaluation marks are particularly linked to this assessment of the bigger global market.

Business growth The process of improving some measure of a firm's success.

Exports and imports

Imports are goods bought from another country. These can either be ready-made goods such as iPads or raw materials to manufacture products in the UK. For example, 36% of UK imports in 2016 were machinery and transport equipment, compared with India where the main import was oil at 34%.

Exports are goods produced in one country which are sold in another country. For example, according to a report by the *Daily Telegraph*, cars contributed 11.2% of exports from the UK to China in 2015.

There are various differences between imports and exports:

- Exports earn money for both the country and the business.
- Imports cost the country and businesses money.
- A **depreciation** in the currency used by an exporter makes the goods more competitive in the global market. This is particularly the case where the exporter is able to source its raw materials within the country in which it is manufacturing. The opposite would apply if the currency appreciated.
- An **appreciation** in the currency weakens the position of exporters but helps importers. Foreign goods become cheaper to purchase and more competitive in the local market. This helps the many retailers that buy from abroad, such as Dixons Carphone, the mobile phone retailer. This retailer sources most of its mobile phones from Asia so with an appreciation of the pound will be able to buy more phones for the same amount of sterling.

> **Exam tip**
>
> Expect to be tested regularly on calculating how to convert one currency to another and the meaning of 'appreciation' and 'depreciation' of a currency.

The link between business specialisation and competitive advantage

Competitive advantage is a sustainable way to keep ahead of your competitors in the long term. **Specialisation** is when a business concentrates on a product or task and in many cases means producing only a small number of products. Specialisation is particularly important when competing in international markets as it can create a competitive advantage for the business and act as a barrier to stop others from entering the market.

> **Exam tip**
>
> The area of competitive advantage can be used in many different questions so you must be familiar with concepts that link to this, such as economies of scale. Examiners love asking questions on competitive advantage.

The links between specialisation and competitive advantage include:

- higher output means total production of goods and services is raised and quality can be improved
- by a business or country using its unique skills and talents in its workforce the output can become more efficient and of far higher quality than elsewhere. Buying pizza in Naples is proof of the value of specialisation (and history)

Imports Commodities, products or services brought in from abroad for sale.

Exports Goods produced in one country and shipped to another country for future sale or trade. The sale of such goods adds to the producing nation's gross output. If used for trade, exports are exchanged for other products or services in other countries.

Currency depreciation The loss of value of a country's currency with respect to one or more foreign reference currencies.

Currency appreciation An increase in the value of one currency in terms of another.

Knowledge check 4

After Britain voted in 2016 to leave the European Union, the pound fell by 12–20% against other currencies. How might that have affected Nissan UK, which exports more than 80% of the cars made in its Sunderland factory?

- a bigger market through specialisation and global trade increase the size of the market, offering opportunities for economies of scale
- competition means lower prices – increased competition acts as an incentive to minimise costs, keep prices down and create a competitive advantage.

Foreign direct investment and the link to business growth

FDI can be used by businesses to achieve the aim of growth. Countries try to attract FDI using strategies such as lower levels of corporation tax, subsidies for the building of factories, and investment in infrastructure such as roads, ports and airports.

Inward FDI involves a foreign business investing in the local economy. In the UK, an example of inward FDI was the French energy company EDF's proposal in 2016 to build a nuclear power station at Hinkley Point in Somerset. According to *The Guardian* newspaper, the Hinkley Point project will cost EDF £18bn. In return the UK government has proposed a 35-year contract to purchase electricity from the power station, valued at approximately £29.7bn, a price that includes a significant profit to EDF.

Outward FDI is where a domestic business expands its operations to a foreign country. For example, Dyson has spent £200m investing in manufacturing in Malaysia.

The ways a business can grow through FDI include:
- through merger, takeover or partnership with a foreign business, in order to quickly enter a market that is not saturated
- relocating production to another country with lower labour and/or raw material costs in order to achieve a competitive advantage.

Factors contributing to increased globalisation

International trade is increasing for a number of reasons.

Reduction of international trade barriers/trade liberalisation. Countries impose trade barriers for many reasons. They include protecting local jobs, allowing new industries to flourish, to protect consumers from particular products or services, and in retaliation for another country's trade practices. **Trade liberalisation** is the removal or reduction of restrictions or barriers to the free exchange of goods between nations. Organisations like the World Trade Organization (WTO) promote free trade between countries, which helps to remove barriers. There are also free trade areas such as the European Union or the Association of Southeast Asian Nations (ASEAN).

Benefits of trade liberalisation include increased economies of scale and greater competition, which can drive down costs and improve quality. Drawbacks include the potential loss of local businesses due to increased competition, infant industries could be lost to foreign competitors, and the vulnerability of some industries to **dumping** by overseas rivals. Dumping occurs when a country has excess stock and so it sells below cost on global markets, causing other producers to become unprofitable.

Inward FDI An investment into a country involving an external or foreign company either investing in or purchasing the goods of a local economy.

Outward FDI A business strategy in which a domestic firm expands its operations to a foreign country via a greenfield investment, merger/acquisition and/or expansion of an existing foreign facility. Employing outward FDI is a natural progression for a company as better business opportunities will be available in foreign countries when domestic markets become too saturated.

Knowledge check 5

Give one reason that a country such as Ireland is so keen on encouraging large multinationals such as Apple to have a large base in their country.

Trade liberalisation Includes the removal or reduction of tariff obstacles, such as duties and surcharges, and non-tariff obstacles, such as licensing rules, quotas and other requirements.

Political change has increased global trade as countries such as China have allowed more businesses to be owned privately. China joined the WTO in 2001. Figure 3 shows the massive impact political change in China has had on exports in the past 30 or so years.

$ billions

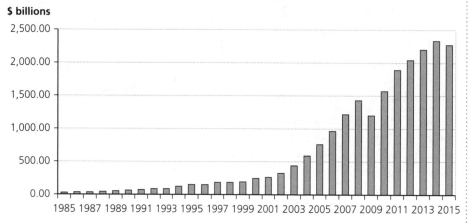

Figure 3 The growth of China's exports 1985–2015 to become the world's number one exporter

Source: World Bank

Reduced cost of transport and communication. Larger cargo ships have resulted in a decrease in the cost of transporting goods between countries. Oil has become cheaper, making global shipping of goods less expensive. Economies of scale mean the cost per item can reduce when operating on a larger scale. Transport improvements also mean that goods and people can travel more quickly.

The internet and mobile technology have allowed greater communication between countries. In India there are 330,000 staff working for call centres for businesses such as British Telecom. People in one country can now order products online or on the telephone to be delivered to a different country.

Increased significance of transnational corporations. A **transnational corporation** is a business that is registered and operates in more than one country at a time but selling the same products. A transnational corporation has its headquarters in one country and operates wholly or partially owned subsidiaries in one or more other countries but with basically the same products offered in each country. A multinational corporation is different in that it still operates in different countries but tends to glocalise its products.

An example of a transnational corporation is British Petroleum, which sells the same petrol products across different countries. Transnational businesses are able to take even greater advantage of globalisation such as significant reductions in sourcing raw materials.

Increased investment flows are the movement of money for the purposes of trade or production. Investment can be made through international markets such as stock exchanges or money markets. Globalisation has facilitated such trading across countries, allowing businesses to more easily access funds to invest in growth in new and emerging markets. Multinational corporations can increase investment flows by building factories and other facilities in other countries. Cross-country mergers, takeovers and partnerships can also increase investment flows.

Migration within and between economies. As transport between countries has become cheaper, quicker and less regulated, globalisation has encouraged workers to move around to find the best jobs and pay for their skill set. Economies such as the US are based on people looking for better opportunities. The relatively high level of migration into the UK became an important factor in the electorate's decision to vote for 'Brexit' in June 2016.

Growth of the global labour force. Countries such as India have low labour costs and (in the IT sector) high skill levels. Offshoring is the practice of basing some of a company's processes or services overseas, so as to take advantage of lower costs. Labour-intensive industries such as clothing can take advantage of cheaper labour costs in emerging economies, in order to lower unit costs.

Structural change is an economic condition that occurs when a country, industry or market changes how it functions or operates. It can affect what countries produce and is normally driven by the quest for increases in the standard of living in the population. For example, according to the Asian Development Bank, agricultural output for India as a percentage of GDP was 29.65% in 1991 but this had reduced to 16.1% in 2015 due to structural change in the economy, moving to a more industrialised economy. In the UK, structural change has meant a move away from manufacturing, but this has been replaced by a strong service sector (for instance, banking).

Protectionism

Protectionism is any attempt by a country, trade bloc or region to impose restrictions on the import of goods and services.

A country may use protectionist measures because of concerns about trade imbalances (too many imports compared with too few exports), to protect jobs or to protect politically sensitive industries such as shipbuilding.

Tariffs

A tariff is a tax or duty that raises the price of imported products. The price rise is likely to reduce demand for the item and also encourage local entrepreneurs to produce more. For example, according to BBC News, in March 2016 the US imposed a 500% tariff on steel being imported from China compared with the 16% tariff charged for importing steel from China to the UK. These tariffs were justified as being a response to unfair 'dumping' by Chinese steel companies selling below cost – perhaps with the intention of driving western steel producers out of business.

Tariffs can also be imposed to protect 'infant' industries, for instance in countries such as India and Malaysia. Tariffs are used to allow for the growth of new industries so that they can gradually take advantage of technological developments and economies of scale which allow them to ultimately become competitive in the global market.

Benefits of imposing tariffs include promoting local industries and products by pricing them below the price of the imported good, increasing government revenue to spend

Migration The movement of people from one place to another.

Knowledge check 6

Give a reason why the dumping of Chinese steel on the UK market risks closing down UK-based steel plants such as Tata Steel. What can Tata Steel do to reduce the effect of this on its global business?

Exam tip

Bear in mind that FDI comprises two things: physical investment and financial investment. Qatar buying Harrods makes little difference to the UK (that is a financial investment) whereas Haribo opening a second factory in Yorkshire in 2010 provided jobs in construction followed by 300 jobs running the factory.

on public services through taxation of the product, discouraging dumping of products and allowing infant industries to flourish. Drawbacks of imposing tariffs include discouraging trade, reducing consumer choice, pushing up prices and restricting competition. The latter may result in home producers becoming inefficient and ultimately may slow the growth of the economy.

Import quotas

Import quotas are quantitative (volume) limits on the level of imports allowed or a limit to the value of imports permitted into a country in a given time period. Often licences are granted to importers to the exclusion of other global businesses. Quotas do not normally bring in any tax revenue for the government.

Benefits of import quotas include keeping the volume of imports unchanged even when demand for imported products increases, the outcome of the quota is certain and precise, local jobs may be created or protected, leading to greater tax revenue, and they can be more flexible than tariffs. Drawbacks of quotas are that they tend to distort international trade as they restrict the amount of imports, they restrict competition, there is no tax revenue from imports, and in some countries there is a risk of corruption from bribes by companies wanting to gain access to the market.

Other trade barriers

Other trade barriers can be implemented.

Government legislation can be imposed in order to both protect consumers and restrict imports. For example, the Convention on International Trade in Endangered Species bans the sale of any objects made from ivory before 1947 and the UK government is looking to make this a total ban. The aim is to stop poaching of endangered species such as elephants. The European Union also bans the use of 1,328 chemicals in cosmetics to protect consumers. However, according to *The Guardian* newspaper, the UK is looking at relaxing the total ban on the use of genetically modified crops in food production, which currently stops US companies importing food made from such substances into the UK.

An advantage of government legislation is that it allows domestic firms to flourish in the market, but it may provoke retaliation from another country if a ban is seen as unfair.

Domestic subsidies are payments to encourage domestic production by lowering their costs. Low- or no-interest loans can be used to fund the dumping of products in overseas markets. Well-known subsidies include the Common Agricultural Policy in the EU, or cotton subsidies for US farmers and farm subsidies introduced by countries such as Russia.

Advantages of subsidies include the protection of local jobs and industries and the reduction of costs to make businesses more competitive in the global market. A disadvantage can be the fact that subsidies can encourage inefficiency and may be seen simply as a protectionist policy, resulting in retaliation.

Import quota A type of protectionist trade restriction that sets a physical limit on the quantity of a good that can be imported into a country in a given period of time. Quotas, like other trade restrictions, are typically used to benefit the producers of a good at the expense of consumers in that economy.

Exam tip

A good way of discussing protectionism in an exam answer is to compare and contrast different methods such as tariffs vs quotas. This helps evaluate the comparative merits and demerits of each.

Trading blocs

A trade bloc is a set of countries which engages in international trade; those countries are usually related through a free trade agreement or other association. The aim of most trade blocs is trade creation as they treat members of the trade bloc more favourably than non-members. There is usually an external **tariff wall**. For example, the European Union has more than 30 separate international trade agreements, including those with countries such as Colombia and South Korea.

Some of these deals are free-trade agreements that involve a reduction in tariff and non-tariff import controls to liberalise trade in goods and services between countries.

Expansion of trading blocs

The number of trading blocs has risen from around 70 in 1990 to more than 300 today, reflecting a switch towards greater intra-regional trade between many of the world's fast-growing emerging market economies. Table 4 shows how trade blocs have expanded across the globe, due to their actual and perceived benefits to countries in an increasingly global and competitive market.

Table 4 Expansion of trading blocs

	Starting date	Main members	Total GDP	Total population 2015 (million)
European Union (EU)	1958	Germany, France, UK (28 in total)	$16,200bn	505
Association of Southeast Asian Nations (ASEAN)	1967	Indonesia, Thailand, Vietnam (10 in total)	$2,431bn	608
MERCOSUR (Spanish for South American common market)	1991	Brazil, Argentina, Uruguay (6 in total)	$3,184bn	303
North American Free Trade Agreement (NAFTA)	1994	US, Canada, Mexico (3 in total)	$20,600bn	484
East African Community (EAC)	2000	Kenya, Tanzania (5 in total)	$147bn	145

Source: World Bank

The WTO permits the existence of trade blocs, provided that they result in lower protection against outside countries than existed before the creation of the trade bloc.

Trade blocs are seen as ways to protect countries, and smaller countries in particular, from increased global competition and to manage market forces for a range of stakeholders, including employees and consumers. Figure 4 shows the adjusted GDP for the world's biggest economies. Germany has significantly lower GDP than China and the US. However, notice the benefit to Germany (and currently the UK) of being part of the European Union trade bloc, raising GDP to almost parity with both countries – size matters.

Tariff wall An amount of money designed to make imports more expensive than domestically produced products. This type of tariff is particularly high and highlights the difficulty foreign businesses have in getting their products past the tariff and on sale in the market.

Knowledge check 7

Give one disadvantage of protecting the countries within a bloc by imposing a tariff wall to those outside the bloc.

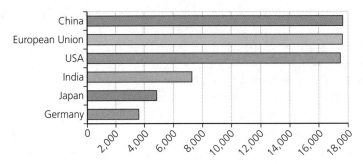

Figure 4 The world's biggest economies (total GDP at purchasing power parity in $bn)

Source: CIA World Factbook 2015

The **European Union** (EU) is a **customs union**, a **single market** and now has a single currency for some of its 28 member states (19 states including Spain and Germany). It started in 1958 and has 28 member states, including the UK (August 2016), and is growing.

Benefits of being part of the EU include the free movement of goods and people within all 28 countries and a single market.

When a country joins the EU it agrees by law (known as a treaty) to unify its national laws with EU law on any goods or services offered across the market. For example, France produces Cassis de Dijon, a blackcurrant liqueur with an alcohol content of 15–20%. German law used to require all fruit liqueurs to have an alcohol content of at least 25%. The effect of the German rule was to keep French liqueurs out of the German market. However, EU rules stated that the German rule interfered with the free movement of goods. Therefore the rule had to be removed, allowing the French liqueur to be sold in Germany.

However, any companies based in countries outside the trade bloc that want to export goods into the EU may still have to pay tariffs. For example, US car makers wanting to export to the EU have to pay a tariff of 10% on every car.

The **ASEAN** trade bloc was established in 1967 and is made up of ten nations with an aggregate economic size of $2.3tn. The aim of ASEAN is to have a free trade area with no tariffs on goods and services and the free flow of skilled workers. The trade bloc has a diverse range of economies, from advanced economies such as Singapore to developing countries like Myanmar.

ASEAN has signed free trade agreements with China, Japan, Korea, India and Australia/New Zealand. China in particular is very important to the success of the trade bloc and has emerged as the number one trading partner. Table 5 shows the success of the trade bloc with Indonesia and Vietnam as examples and the UK to give a comparison.

Customs union A group of states that has agreed to charge the same import duties as each other and usually to allow free trade between themselves.

Single market An association of countries trading with each other without restrictions or tariffs.

Table 5 Growth in GDP per capita at purchasing power parity to $US

	1990	2000	2015	% increase in GDP 1990–2015
Indonesia*	$2,892	$4,601	$11,035	281%
Vietnam*	$6,755	$12,798	$26,891	298%
India	$1,148	$2,020	$5,730	399%
China	$980	$2,195	$13,400	1,267%
UK	$17,985	$27,340	$38,657	115%

*Italic = member of ASEAN

Source: World Bank 2015

NAFTA, which includes Mexico, the US and Canada, was established in 1994. While the US and Canada are highly developed countries, Mexico is officially classed as a middle-income country (GDP per head is only around a quarter of that in the US). NAFTA's aims are to reduce trade barriers and encourage free and standardised trade of goods and services.

However, the US has seen a reduction in manufacturing jobs, with multinational companies such as Nissan basing their factories in Mexico due to lower costs. Mexico has seen the type of work available change to more part-time jobs even though unemployment in cities has reduced. Mexico has also seen its agricultural sector suffer due to increased competition from the US and Canada after the Mexican government withdrew subsidies from farmers.

Impact on business of trading blocs

The impact on businesses of trading blocs depends on whether the business is trading within the bloc or outside of the bloc.

For businesses trading within the bloc the impact includes market access with fewer or no barriers to trade other than those imposed by competition, access to a larger workforce with a greater skill set, and protection from cheaper imports from outside the trade bloc.

Businesses trading outside the bloc are likely to have higher costs as the result of tariffs being imposed, and costs may be higher due to having to meet the legal requirements of trading within the bloc. It may also be difficult to compete due to local competitors being subsidised.

With the UK voting in June 2016 to leave the EU, it will be interesting to see whether the advantages of leaving outweigh the disadvantages. The advantages and disadvantages of trading blocs are outlined in Table 6.

Table 6 Advantages and drawbacks of trading blocs to businesses

Advantages to businesses of trading blocs	Drawbacks to businesses of trading blocs
Free movement of goods between members gives the potential to create a large 'single market'	Competition increases due to freer trade, so those with monopoly power may find it competed away
External tariff walls insulate the business from competition from another part of the world	To create a single market, new rules and regulations may be agreed, including minimum wage rates
As trade grows between neighbours, it becomes economic (and necessary) for governments to provide infrastructure support	The availability of easily accessed neighbouring markets may reduce enterprise in relation to distant but dynamic ones such as China
The advantages become much greater if there is free movement of labour as well as free movement of goods	Within a geographically proximate bloc, there may be common factors that together become common problems, e.g. low commodity prices

Knowledge check 8

Give one reason why emerging economies in particular felt the need to form trade blocs.

Exam tip

Trade blocs are bound to feature at some point on your exam as they have become a significant issue for global businesses. In particular, expect the exit of the UK from the EU to be a fertile area for exam questions.

Knowledge check 9

Give a reason why a trade bloc such as the EU could be seen to be failing to promote free trade globally.

Summary

After studying this topic, you should be able to:
- describe globalisation and its relationship to growth rate and growing economies
- discuss the implications of economic growth for businesses and individuals
- identify, explain and discuss the indicators of growth in an economy
- explain the differences between exports and imports and the effects an appreciation or depreciation of a currency has on businesses that export or import
- understand the link between business specialisation and competitive advantage
- explain foreign direct investment and its link to business growth and the factors that lead to increased globalisation
- discuss the benefits and drawbacks of protectionism, including tariffs and quotas
- explain what trade blocs are and discuss the impact on business of the expansion of trading blocs

Global markets and business expansion

Conditions that prompt trade

There are some factors that force businesses to consider selling and/or basing production abroad and there are significant opportunities for selling to overseas markets.

Push factors

Push factors are reasons a business may want to grow outside of the domestic country in which it currently operates. The factors are linked to the business's domestic market.

High levels of domestic competition mean a business will try to move into markets that are undeveloped and/or have less powerful competitors. This can happen particularly to small to medium-sized businesses when multinational corporations enter a domestic market.

Saturated markets are the point at which a market is no longer generating new demand for a firm's products, due to competition, decreased need, obsolescence, or some other factor. Businesses will look for growth in overseas markets where there are similar characteristics, for example demographic trends and GDP per capita. An example of a UK saturated market is the grocery market, where Tesco attempted to expand into China, Thailand and the US.

Pull factors

Pull factors are the opportunities a business may see for expansion into a foreign market. The factors are linked to the foreign market in which the business wishes to operate.

Economies of scale are present when unit costs fall as output rises. Globalisation has meant a rise in opportunities for international businesses to reduce unit costs by increasing sales volumes to new and emerging markets, thus being able to buy the raw materials to make the products in bulk. Businesses have also moved production

Push factors Things that influence a business to start to operate in another market. Often businesses look to another country when operations in their current market are difficult. This can include a saturated market and products coming to the end of the product life cycle.

Pull factors Things that tempt a business to operate in another market. Pull factors include lower levels of competition or an untapped market of customers.

to new markets where costs such as wages are significantly cheaper than in their domestic market. According to *The Wall Street Journal*, towards the end of 2016 Ford announced that it would be building a new car production plant in Mexico where average earnings are $12,000 compared with $57,000 in the US.

Risk spreading is a benefit from moving into overseas markets in order to reduce the dependence on the home market. A wet summer in Britain does not worry Wall's as it sells its ice cream in lots of overseas markets.

Possibility of offshoring and outsourcing

Offshoring means a business getting work done in a different country. Figure 5 shows one reason a business may offshore part of its business, such as production. For example, Hyundai, the car maker, has offshored the production of its cars to the Czech Republic from South Korea, one reason being low wage costs compared with those of domestic workers (a saving of £2.50 per hour per worker in 2016).

The advantages of offshoring include access to lower unit costs, access to more specialised suppliers and services, and economies of scale from operating in larger international markets. Disadvantages include the fact that public and employee relations may suffer due to moving jobs abroad, higher costs such as training, poor customer service, and risks to legal protection for key business information such as patents and brands.

Offshoring When a company moves various operations to another country for reasons such as lower labour costs or more favourable economic conditions in that other country.

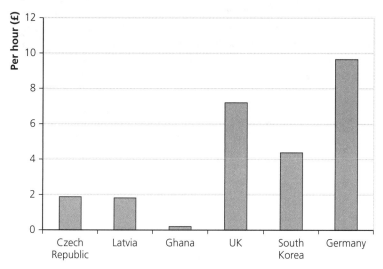

Figure 5 National minimum wages in selected countries, 2016

Source: wage indicator.org

Outsourcing means a business gets another business to do the work for it, either in the same or in a different country.

A key difference between offshoring and outsourcing is that the offshored element of the business is still part of the same global business but outsourcing means a completely separate business takes over the work. Outsourcing is often done to take advantage of another business's specialised skills, cost effectiveness and worker flexibility. For example, Apple outsources the production of its iPhone to Foxconn in China.

Outsourcing A practice used by companies to reduce costs by transferring portions of work to outside suppliers rather than completing it internally. Outsourcing is an effective cost-saving strategy when used properly.

Advantages of outsourcing are similar to those of offshoring and also include the business being able to focus on its own core areas, and savings on spending on new production facilities. Disadvantages of outsourcing are also similar to those of offshoring but also include a potential loss of customer service and brand recognition as outsourcing businesses may work for many other different customers.

Extending the product life cycle by selling in multiple markets

According to the product life cycle, a product will peak in its maturity stage and then start to decline, resulting in less profit. An extension strategy used by businesses is to introduce the product to a new international market, effectively extending the life of the product. This multiple market approach is used by many multinational corporations. For example, according to *Car and Driver* magazine, VW stopped selling its Beetle in 1978 with the exception of two markets, Mexico and Brazil, where it continued selling the car, particularly to be used as a taxi, until 2002. The product has since seen a revival with a new product which VW released in 1997 to the European and North American market. It has since become a global product.

Advantages of selling products in multiple markets include continued profitable returns, potential economies of scale due to selling large numbers of the product, and the potential to develop a new and loyal customer base for current and future products. Disadvantages include the risks of operating in new markets, such as language barriers, increased costs due to exporting the product, and the expense of marketing campaigns to raise awareness of the product among new customers. Products may also need to be adapted to the local market or may actually be unsaleable in their current form, meaning increased costs from further product development.

Assessment of a country as a market

Market attractiveness is a measure of the potential value of a particular market in a country. It can include short-term or long-term profit and growth rate of the market. A range of tools can be used to assess market attractiveness for a country, such as the Boston Matrix (Student Guide 1), PESTLE and Porter's Five Forces analysis (Student Guide 3). Market research should be undertaken by any business assessing the attractiveness of a new market in a country.

There are several key issues to consider when assessing the market attractiveness.

Levels and growth of disposable income

Changes in **disposable income** are believed to have a strong relationship over time with the level of consumer spending on goods and services, which is why assessment of the growth over time is a key measure of a country's market. Levels can be measured using GDP per capita. For example, in the Czech Republic GDP per capita in 2003 was $9,741 compared with $19,563 in 2014, a 101% increase. This may indicate to a business that the market in the Czech Republic today is more attractive for a business to enter than it was in 2003. However, to assess the country more accurately, a comparison with other economies may put the figures into context with a look at the trends over a period of time. Figure 6 shows a comparison of three Eastern

Knowledge check 10

Give one reason why some UK multinationals are bringing back to the UK outsourced manufacturing and services currently undertaken in emerging economies such as India.

Exam tip

An exam question may not directly ask you about push or pull factors so you need to be able to assess the evidence you are given to spot the issues and particularly home in on the specific factors that need to be evaluated.

Disposable income
Household income after the deduction of taxes and the addition of benefits.

European countries. You can see that Poland has better growth in GDP per capita than the Czech Republic, although the actual per capita amount is still higher in the Czech Republic.

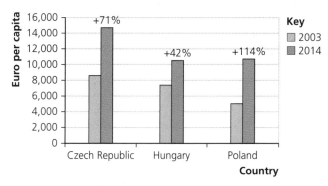

Figure 6 GDP per capita in three Eastern European countries in 2003 and 2014

Source: Eurostat 2015

So the Czech Republic is reasonably well off, but is the economy healthy and stable? For that, it's good to check the country's trading position (exports minus imports) and its debt level. Table 7 shows that the Czech Republic's external trade is far healthier than the UK's. UK net debt as a percentage of GDP is also higher at 79.1% compared with the Czech Republic's of 43.5%. It will depend on the type of products that a business is planning to export as to which of the Eastern European countries it wishes to target based on this data, but all three appear to be reasonably stable countries to expand into.

Table 7 How stable is the country's economic position?

	Current account balance (as % of GDP)	Government net debt (as a % of GDP)
Czech Republic	+1.6	43.5
Hungary	+4.8	78.2
Poland	−1.8	45.6
UK	−4.8	79.1

Source: Courtesy of the Central Intelligence Agency, *CIA World Factbook* 2015

Ease of doing business depends on issues such as how quickly a business can start up, access to credit, taxation system, enforcing contracts, and quality of infrastructure such as electricity access. An extract from the World Economic Forum's (WEF) annual assessment of these key factors for 2016 is given in Table 8, showing the performance of Hungary, Poland and the Czech Republic.

Table 8 Ease of doing business in three Eastern European countries

	Hungary	Poland	Czech Republic
Days to start a business	5	30	15
Days for construction permit	179	156	247
Total tax rate (% of profit)	48.3	40.3	50.4

Source: World Bank 2016

It is quickest to set up a business in Hungary, according to Table 8, while Poland has the lowest tax rate, which is likely to be the most important factor in this set of data.

Infrastructure

It is important to consider infrastructure such as roads, internet and electricity supply. In 2016 the Czech Republic was better on most matters than Poland or Hungary. For example, railways were rated 4.5 out of 7 in the Czech Republic compared with only 2.9 in Poland, so if deliveries of goods such as fresh food just in time was important to a business, this would be a better bet than the other two countries.

Political stability

Political stability is an absence of excessive fluctuations in the economy. An economy with fairly constant output, growth and low and stable inflation would be considered economically stable. Countries with less stable governments tend to be less attractive and riskier for a business to operate in.

Table 9 Problematic factors for doing business in three Eastern European countries

Percentage saying it is a big problem	Czech Republic	Hungary	Poland
Policy instability	9.1%	15.1%	3.3%
Tax regulations	8.0%	11.0%	23.2%
Labour regulations	9.0%	1.0%	15.5%
Government bureaucracy	18.6%	10.3%	14.6%
Corruption	16.3%	13.0%	3.4%

Source: World Economic Forum 2015

Table 9 shows that 15.1% of business people in Hungary felt policy instability was the biggest problem in doing business whereas in Poland 3.3% saw this as a problem. This means a business looking at Hungary as a potential market may find it less attractive as the government appears to change its rules for business rather too often. In the UK, bribes by businesses are now a criminal offence, so countries with high levels of corruption will be of particular concern in terms of attractiveness.

Exchange rates can directly affect a business and determine how much of one currency has to be given up in order to buy a specific amount of another currency. A stronger pound makes it cheaper to pay for imports, but exports will seem more expensive to overseas customers.

The problem is that exchange rates tend to fluctuate a lot so it is difficult to establish attractiveness of entering a market in a country based on this factor alone. However, by looking at historical data on a currency a business may be able to decide when it is best to enter a new market.

Figure 7 shows the value of pound sterling to the Czech crown for two years up to 2016. A UK business looking to export to the Czech Republic would experience a variation in local currency between £1 = 29 crowns to £1 = 39 crowns. In August 2016 the exchange rate varied again, with £1 = 31 crowns. For a UK business wanting to buy, say, a Czech chocolate factory, the more crowns to the pound, the better. If the factory cost 30m crowns and the exchange rate was £1 = 30 Cr, then the factory would cost £1m exactly. If the pound appreciated to 39 crowns, the factory would cost 30m/39 Cr = £0.769m. That's a saving of £231,000!

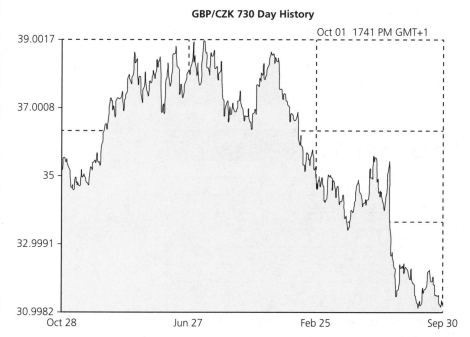

Figure 7 Pound sterling vs Czech crown, 2014–2016

Source: www.exchangerates.org.uk

Knowledge check 11

Give a possible reason why niche market products such as Jaguar cars are doing so well in the Chinese market.

Exam tip

It is likely you will need to assess the country as a market from the evidence given to you in the exam. You need to read the evidence carefully, picking out competing issues so that you can give a good evaluation for the business or industry which is the focus of the question.

On the issue of exchange rates, a good way to remember the effects of the appreciation of a currency is SPICED: Strong Pound: Imports Cheaper, Exports Dearer.

Assessment of a country as a production location

Production is defined as the total amount of output produced in a time period (Student Guide 2). The more that can be produced in a specific period of time, the more efficient the business becomes in using its resources.

Production in terms of assessment of a country takes on a wider definition to include services such as staff answering customer queries in call centres. Investment appraisal techniques such as payback are covered in Student Guide 3, in terms of the financial assessment of such a move.

There are other factors a business needs to take into account. **Costs of production** need to be compared to current and future possible locations in order to assess the value of a move. The Boston Consulting Group (BCG) Global Manufacturing Cost-Competitiveness Index measured changes in direct manufacturing costs from 2004 to 2014 among the world's top 25 exporting economies. The index develops

Production A process of workers combining various material inputs and know-how in order to make something for consumption by the customer, known as the output.

competitiveness scores based on manufacturing wages, productivity and energy costs, using the US as the base point of 100. Labour costs take into account the productivity of the labour. Table 10 shows that Taiwan was 7.7% more cost competitive than the US in 2004 but this figure had dropped to 2.8% in 2014. Meanwhile, the UK managed to become slightly more competitive from 2004 to 2014.

Table 10 Boston Consulting Group data on manufacturing costs in selected countries relative to the cost of manufacturing in the US

Country	Indexed manufacturing costs 2004 (US = 100)	Indexed manufacturing costs 2014 (US = 100)
Czech Republic	96.6	106.7
Canada	104	115.4
Taiwan	92.3	97.2
UK	107.4	108.7
South Korea	98.7	102.4
India	112.7	111.5
Brazil	96.8	123.6

Source: www.bcgperspectives.com

However, labour costs are not always the most important factor when considering production in another country. For example, BMW decided to base the new Mini production in the UK even though labour costs would be more expensive than, say, India. Car production is capital rather than labour intensive, so labour costs are a small part of the cost of a car, and the brand was associated with the UK.

Skills and availability of the labour force are other significant factors. A business must consider the level of literacy and skills of the local workforce. According to McKinsey Global Institute (www.mckinsey.com), at the end of 2015 there was a skills shortage across the global economy, for instance a projected 40m fewer workers with university or higher education and an extra 13% more demand for such skills. The key is to identify the country that has the right skills available for the production the business is looking to relocate.

Infrastructure refers to the facilities that support everyday economic activity – for example, roads, phone lines and gas pipes. Businesses need to consider the availability of an infrastructure that supports the production process, such as good access to power and a reliable road network. The importance of infrastructure, such as the availability of electricity, has been discussed under the attractiveness of the market.

Location in a trade bloc is another consideration. Trade blocs such as the EU are a form of economic integration and increasingly are shaping the pattern of world trade and production. Table 4 gives a summary of important trade blocs with more detailed discussion of each. Businesses have located production within trade blocs for numerous reasons including no tariffs or quotas as products are not treated as imports, and glocalisation of products to meet local needs. For example, Japanese car manufacturers such as Nissan and Toyota have invested heavily in production in the UK as a way of selling cars competitively within the EU. (Brexit presents them with some awkward decisions.)

Government incentives are rewards or inducements offered to businesses to start trading in a country. These include tax breaks, grants and cheap loans. For example, for the Hinkley Point nuclear power station in Somerset, EDF, the French energy company, is being offered high, guaranteed payments for each megawatt of power produced. These payments are far above the normal rate, to entice EDF to invest the $18bn in setting up the power station (*The Guardian*, 28 July 2016).

Ease of doing business measures how straightforward it is for a new business to start production in a country. The World Bank conducts an annual survey, 'Doing business', which measures factors such as getting electricity, the ease of starting a business and exporting, to create a ranking of the best and worst countries for setting up a company. For example, the 2016 report rates Singapore as the easiest, with Eritrea at the bottom of the rankings at 189. The UK is ranked 6th, Mexico 38th and India 130th.

Political stability has been covered earlier and raises the same issues for production.

Natural resources are materials or substances occurring in nature which can be exploited for economic gain – in other words, raw materials like iron ore, coal or large forests or lakes. In Iceland, water heated by volcanic activity means the country creates the vast majority of its power and heat for business for free. A business may decide to move production to reduce costs of power or raw materials.

Likely return on investment means a performance measure used to evaluate the potential profitability of an investment or to compare the returns from a number of different investments. This is likely to be a measure such as average rate of return (ARR) or net present value (NPV). Either method would give a solid basis for making an investment decision (see Student Guide 3). Clearly the business and its investors will need to be sure that the investment will make a satisfactory profit and will look at issues such as opportunity cost and the risk versus return.

Reasons for global mergers or joint ventures

A **global merger** is an agreement between two companies from different countries to join forces permanently (merger issues are covered in Student Guide 3). A **joint venture** is a separate business entity created by two or more parties, involving shared ownership, returns and risks.

> Joint venture A business arrangement in which two or more parties agree to pool their resources for the purpose of accomplishing a specific task. This task can be a new project or any other business activity.

Joint ventures are different from mergers in that the risks and returns of the business formed as the joint venture are shared by the parties involved. These parties are usually looking to benefit from complementary strengths and resources brought to the venture, as well as sharing the risks and rewards.

Joint ventures or global mergers are undertaken for a number of reasons.

Spreading risk over different countries means that any setup costs are shared by the joint venture or the newly merged company. Expertise can also be shared, again lowering risks in different global markets. Mergers help increase growth quickly for a business, which may be particularly important in emerging economies, where size may help ensure the success.

Knowledge check 12

Give a reason why NAFTA member Mexico has seen a large increase in US and global car manufacturers moving production to the nation since joining the trade bloc.

Exam tip

Be careful not to confuse a country as a production centre and as a potential market. Your answers must be tailored precisely to the question set. All exam answers are produced using job production, never by a fudged version of batch or flow production. In other words, the examiner will make sure they look carefully over each student's answers rather than rush through them.

Global merger Voluntary amalgamation of two businesses which operate in foreign markets on roughly equal terms into one new legal entity. Mergers are brought about by the exchange of stocks and shares from the old businesses for the stock of the new business.

Entering new market/trade blocs can be achieved in three ways: organic growth through starting from scratch, through a merger or takeover and through a joint venture. In trade blocs such as the EU or other western markets all three options are usually possible. However, in emerging economies, businesses from foreign countries are often allowed to enter a market only as a joint venture. For example, in China not only are joint ventures more likely to gain government approval than a merger but they also bring the knowledge and experience of a local partner. Joint ventures exploit market knowledge, win preferential treatment and manufacturing capability, and acquire the general business know-how. Joint ventures are also allowed to buy and own land, which is more difficult for merged companies, or those multinationals that want to set up from scratch.

According to BBC News (November 2014), in India McDonald's created a joint venture in 2010 with a national fast-food business run by entrepreneur Amit Jatia. This saw the introduction of unique vegetarian dishes, which transformed the fast-food giant's success in the emerging market, growing sales by 200%.

Acquiring national/international brand names/patents is an important means to global success for multinational corporations, as acquiring national brands can provide instant market share. The right brand might also provide an entry point to more markets globally. For example, Tata from India has acquired Jaguar Land Rover, which has seen growth in emerging markets such as China.

Patents for technology such as the Dyson hair dryer are often illegally reproduced and sold in emerging markets such as China. According to *Wired* magazine (August 2016), estimates suggest that up to 10% of goods worldwide are counterfeit, which is lost revenue for the businesses.

Patent A limited legal monopoly granted by a government to an individual or firm to make, use and sell its invention and to exclude others from doing so.

Joint ventures and mergers can often help a multinational corporation protect global revenue through use of national law as well as being able to acquire technical expertise that can be used in other markets. For example, Middleby, a US company in the food service equipment industry, acquired UK company AGA Rangemaster together with any patents associated with the niche market cookers (*Shropshire Star*, 14 September 2015). Middleby therefore gain growth in the numerous markets in which AGA operates and the added expertise to positively improve its own products.

Securing resources/supplies of an economic or productive factor required to accomplish an activity is important. Resources include land and raw materials. China has made strategic purchases of resources in countries such as Sierra Leone to ensure a steady supply of industrial essentials such as iron ore.

Where a business is accessing resources that are obtained unethically (Student Guide 3), a business may need to take over the supplier in order to maintain the business's reputation and customer loyalty.

Maintaining/increasing global competitiveness means a business's ability to compete with others in the international market. All firms in the same market are chasing the same thing, so the concept of competitiveness is a moving target. The complacent business that has enjoyed advantages in the past soon finds that it is overtaken by hungrier, fast-moving competitors.

Table 11 shows the advantages and disadvantages of mergers and joint ventures.

Table 11 Global mergers vs joint ventures

Mergers	Joint ventures
Advantages	**Advantages**
• A reduction in unit costs through economies of scale which can translate into greater profit margins. • The spreading of risks where products are different, meaning profits can be maintained even if some products are not performing as well as others. • A reduction in competition if a rival is taken over, giving the business more market power and the potential to increase product prices without losing demand. • The addition of new skills and competences which can translate into innovation and ultimately more profit.	• Entering related businesses that previously presented high barriers to entry. • Gaining access to expertise without the need to hire more staff. • Using existing technologies and patents developed by other companies. • Sharing the risk of high gearing but uncertain ventures. • Establishing a presence in new, untapped markets, including international opportunities.
Disadvantages	**Disadvantages**
• The cost of buying up another business can be measured in billions of pounds. Often such takeovers are financed by debt, leading to risky levels of gearing. • Diseconomies of scale can lead to higher unit costs. • Clashes of cultures between different businesses can occur, reducing the integration's effectiveness and potentially affecting quality and productivity and ultimately profits. • Redundancy of workers, particularly managers, may affect the overall motivation of the new business, ultimately driving down profits.	• Setting unrealistic objectives that may not be completely clear in advance and not aligned to a common goal. • Coping with differing cultures, management styles and working relationships in each business. • Managing communication with senior managers and employees in both companies so that there is consistent understanding of the joint venture's objectives. • Making poor tactical decisions caused by a misunderstanding of each company's roles.

> **Exam tip**
>
> Remember to draw on your knowledge of mergers and takeovers from Theme 3 to help with a global perspective on this issue.

Global competitiveness

Global competitiveness is the ability of a business, usually a multinational corporation, to perform better than its rivals across markets in different countries. This can be achieved through performance on price and quality or customers' perception of these factors.

For example, according to *The Guardian* newspaper, in the fast-food market in the US McDonald's had the biggest sales of $35.4bn in 2015 but sales globally fell 1.7%, and 4.4% in the US market. Pizza Hut ranks ninth in the US market for sales of fast food but is increasing its sales globally. To maintain competitiveness businesses are constantly evolving and innovating, which Pizza Hut appears to have done better than McDonald's.

The impact of movements in exchange rates

The exchange rate decides how much currency has to be spent by a business in order to buy a specific amount of another currency. Exchange rate movements are fluctuations in value between currencies, which can result in losses to businesses that import and export goods and to investors.

> **Knowledge check 13**
>
> Why do some emerging economies make a joint venture a condition of trade within the country for multinational corporations considering entering the market? What is the benefit for the local partner of a joint venture?

Global competitiveness The set of institutions, policies and factors that determines the level of a country's productivity. The more competitive economy is one that is likely to grow faster over time.

Exchange rates have different effects on different businesses. One impact of a low exchange rate on a business that has a large amount of exports is that the products will be less expensive to purchase for overseas customers. For example, Rolls-Royce, the manufacturer of aircraft engines, sells its products to Boeing, the US aircraft manufacturer. On 23 June 2016, before the UK voted to leave the EU, £1 bought $1.48. An aircraft engine costing £1m would cost Boeing $1.48m. However, after the vote to leave the EU there were significant downward exchange rate fluctuations, meaning any export sales completed by Rolls-Royce would actually cost Boeing less. In this example, based on the 26 August 2016 exchange rate of $1.33 to the £1, the same £1m engine would now cost Boeing $1.33m, a saving of $150,000.

Therefore, exporting businesses are more competitive when the exchange rate is low. This is because the lower exchange rate makes exports cheaper to buy.

An impact of a low exchange rate on businesses that have competition from imports is that the imports will go up in price so competition will weaken. This means domestic businesses should be able to gain market share from importers. For example, importing steel from China became more expensive after the Brexit vote led to a depreciation of the pound. So British-made steel became more attractive for UK car manufacturers.

The impact of a high exchange rate is the exact opposite. An appreciation in the pound against other currencies means exporters will find it harder to compete with other businesses as their products will be more expensive in terms of the local currency. However, importers will find their products more expensive than those of domestic competitors, who will now find it easier to compete for sales.

Exporters will look at ways to minimise the negative impacts of exchange rate fluctuations by strengthening product differentiation and branding. Customers who want a Burberry raincoat buy that raincoat whether the price is £1,600 or £1,800.

Competitive advantage

A **competitive advantage** is a benefit gained over competitors by offering consumers greater value, either by means of lower prices or by providing greater benefits and service that justifies higher prices.

Competitive advantage is covered in Student Guide 3 using Porter's Strategic Matrix. For global competitive advantage this includes **cost competitiveness**, which means the differences in unit costs between competitors. The key to competitive advantage is to ensure unit costs are lower than those of competitors, achieving **cost leadership**. With this strategy, the objective is to become the lowest-cost producer in the industry.

Cost leadership can be achieved in a number of ways, including a high-productivity workforce, high-capacity utilisation, lean and efficient distribution, lean production and innovative technology. For Germany, which has productivity rates about 30% higher than in the UK, the secret has been heavy investment in training and new technology.

Outsourcing is another method of gaining cost competitiveness, at least in the short term. By giving the work to specialist (or low-wage) suppliers, the business can gain lower unit costs and a competitive advantage. Companies such as Sports Direct outsource warehouse work to agencies that employ staff on minimum-wage, 'zero-hours' contracts.

Competitive advantage Conditions that allow a company or country to produce a good or service at a lower price or in a more desirable fashion for customers. These conditions allow the productive business or country to generate more sales than its competition. Competitive advantages are attributed to a variety of factors, including cost structure, brand and quality of product.

Cost leadership The lowest cost of operation in the industry.

Offshoring is another method of gaining cost competitiveness, the main difference being that the business keeps full control of the function it is basing overseas. For example, according to the news site Bloomberg, Mercedes decided to offshore production for North American cars to Mexico in 2014 with a $1.4bn site, which meant a saving in unit costs due to cheaper raw materials, land, corporation tax and labour costs. However, Mercedes retains total control of the facility, including quality of the cars made there.

Competitive advantage through **product differentiation** is where the global business aims to make a product more attractive by contrasting its unique qualities in terms of price, quality or service with other competing products. This can be achieved in a number of ways, including establishing a strong brand image for a good or service, making the unique selling point of a good or service clear, or through better design or innovation. Businesses producing products in higher-cost economies such as the UK cannot easily compete on price with emerging economies such as China; instead they look to differentiate their product on quality.

Skills shortages and the impact on international competitiveness

A lack of ability to recruit skilled workers could lead to a decline in competitiveness as global businesses will not be able to take advantage of lower unit costs and/or higher-quality products. This will be a particular risk for businesses that take the differentiated approach, such as products that rely on a high level of expertise and craftsmanship. This risk can be reduced by good corporate planning to ensure skills are available to create a competitive advantage and this may involve outsourcing or offshoring.

Exam tip

Make sure you look at a range of factors on global competitiveness when evaluating the issue from a business perspective. Do not just accept that cheaper costs make a business more competitive; there may be hidden costs such as negative customer perceptions of moving to areas of the world with low pay.

Knowledge check 14

Give a reason why discounters such as Aldi are able to outcompete UK supermarkets such as Tesco. What could Tesco do to reduce the impact of this fierce competition?

Summary

After studying this topic, you should be able to:
- describe push and pull factors that prompt global business expansion
- discuss the benefits of outsourcing and offshoring
- identify, explain and discuss the indicators of growth in an economy
- explain and assess the attractiveness of a country as a market for a business
- explain and assess a country as a production location for a business
- explain the reasons for global mergers and joint ventures, including the comparative advantages and disadvantages
- explain the impact of movements in exchange rates and skills shortages on global competitiveness and competitive advantages

■ Global marketing

Global marketing is the choice of marketing strategy to find a fit between an individual company's objectives and its unique market position. Global marketing is a strategy that attempts to increase sales through promotion and advertisements to the international market. Increasingly, large businesses have a global presence. Even companies doing business within their homes can market and attract business internationally, for example via the internet.

Marketing

Marketing is the process of understanding customers and finding ways to provide products or services which customers demand. Marketing is dealt with in Student Guide 1.

Global marketing strategy and global localisation

Marketing strategies explain how the marketing function fits in with the overall strategy for a business. Table 12 gives an example of a business's strategy and how this might link into a global marketing strategy.

Table 12 Example business strategies related to global marketing strategies

Business strategy	Example global marketing strategy
Grow sales	Launch new products in different markets Start selling current products into overseas markets
Increase profits	Increase selling prices in overseas markets Reduce the amount spent on global advertising
Build customer awareness	Invest more in global advertising

Multinational corporations such as Coca-Cola and McDonald's use the same global marketing strategies in each market in which they operate, which has the advantage of economies of scale across global markets, called **global brands**. This would be a transnational corporation approach which is also used by Rolls-Royce cars, Chanel handbags and Tiffany jewellery, all luxury products.

However, businesses increasingly have found that markets are more sophisticated and competition is more intense, so **glocalisation** has become a preferred approach for many global marketing strategies. An example of a failed global marketing strategy was the launch of Toyota's Fiera car across a number of global markets, including Puerto Rico. Unfortunately, unknown to Toyota, the word translated to 'ugly old woman', so the marketing strategy failed and the result was a negative impact on the brand and sales.

Glocalisation means the business thinks globally about its overall marketing strategy but adapts it to meet the needs of the local market. Hence the phrase 'think global, act local'. For example, the 'Milky Way' chocolate bar in the UK is known as '3 Musketeers' in the US. Similarly, Burger King has a different range of food in India as most of the local population will not eat beef. Most mass market products are glocalised to ensure the brands are attractive locally. Only a few brands are able to be truly international, such as Wall's Magnum (worth more than $1 billion in annual sales around the globe).

Global marketing
A product strategy to increase sales through promotion and advertisements to the international market. It focuses the 4Ps – price, promotion, place and product – on a range of foreign markets.

Marketing strategy
A process to allow a business to focus limited resources on the best opportunities to increase sales and thereby achieve a sustainable competitive advantage.

Table 13 outlines the strength of global brands compared with localising brands.

Table 13 Global versus glocal branding

Strength of global brands	Strength of localising brands
Huge sales provide mass production and large economies of scale	Tailoring to local tastes and habits boosts market share
Many promotional tools are global and can be cost effective only if brands are sold globally	Local buyers associate more with the product as they believe it is locally produced
Global scale means stronger negotiating power with retailers	Localised brands can mean local production, with cost savings and a more environmentally friendly image for the business

Different marketing approaches

Businesses can adopt the following approaches to global marketing.

In the **ethnocentric/domestic approach** businesses see overseas markets as almost identical to the domestic market, with local marketing and promotion of the product reproduced overseas. There is no adaptation of the product to the overseas market and in order for this to be a successful approach the markets need to be similar. For example, Nissan started out using an ethnocentric approach to car sales where all cars in overseas markets were exactly the same as those in the local Japanese domestic market.

Among the benefits of an ethnocentric approach is the fact that standardisation provides significant economies of scale and much lower marketing costs as there is little or no research required for new markets. A drawback is the risk of losing sales as the business is not market orientated.

Using the **international/polycentric approach** businesses adapt their marketing strategy to the local market, providing products tailored to that market. This is because the business believes the overseas market is distinct from the domestic market. For example, Pizza Hut in Japan has pizza toppings of squid and seaweed and in South Korea it offers a crust stuffed with sweet potato to satisfy local customer tastes.

A benefit of this approach includes a likely increase in sales and local brand loyalty due to the market orientation of the product. A drawback is that average product costs will increase due to new product development, market research and a reduction in economies of scale.

The **mixed/geocentric approach** is a fusion of the polycentric and ethnocentric approaches, trying to manage any matters that can be approached globally from an ethnocentric approach and dealing with local needs from a polycentric perspective.

This approach takes the benefits of polycentric and ethnocentric to gain the best of both and hence is the best approach for businesses to take. For example, Coca-Cola can operate an ethnocentric approach in markets such as the UK and the US and benefit from economies of scale, but a polycentric approach in places like India, where customers have less money to spend; hence smaller cans are sold at cheaper prices. This approach fits a strategy of glocalisation.

Knowledge check 15

Give a reason why a luxury brand such as Chanel handbags would adopt an ethnocentric approach to marketing. Why has this not worked for McDonald's?

The benefits are the same as the polycentric and the ethnocentric approaches. The biggest drawback is that it will not always be clear which is the correct strategy to choose for different markets, which could lead to the wrong approach, invoking the drawbacks of either the ethnocentric or the polycentric perspective already discussed.

Application and adaptation of the marketing mix

The **marketing mix** needs to be applied carefully in order to meet the requirements of customers in all markets, which is a challenge for businesses. The orientation of products should concentrate on increasing sales and becoming a more recognised brand in the country in which the business has newly set up.

Price strategies that have worked in other economies such as western markets are unlikely to be successful in emerging and undeveloped economies where economic development is low. Therefore, pricing strategies need to be tailored to local customers. In some cases, this means pricing low, such as Coca-Cola's 10p can in India. In other cases, it means pricing high, such as the Land Rover Evoque, selling well in China despite double the UK price tag.

Place is how products are distributed to the market and customers. See Student Guide 1.

With developed economies businesses use many methods of distribution to allow customers to access their products and services. For example, customers shopping for groceries in the UK can place an order on their smartphone and have the items delivered to their door. Businesses entering technologically advanced markets therefore need to ensure they are continually providing new methods of distribution as part of their marketing mix. In emerging economies such as India, the grocery market is dominated by millions of small, independent stores. Furthermore, the country's infrastructure would make it hard to offer the delivery speed of Amazon in the US and the UK. This means Amazon needs to adapt its global distribution strategy to local variations in the market.

Promotion needs to consider local technology and customers' sophistication and preferences. In Germany, traditional channels such as TV are still the preferred medium, while in the UK, social media has become a crucial tool for promoting products. But China has gone digital even faster than the UK – in China, e-commerce and social media are critical.

Applying Ansoff's Matrix to global markets

Ansoff's Matrix is a strategic marketing planning tool that links a business's marketing strategy with its general strategic direction. It presents four alternative growth strategies as a table, known as a matrix. The heart of Ansoff's theory is the relationship between risk and reward. This is covered in detail in Student Guide 3.

Clearly, launching a product/business into a global market involves risks, so Ansoff's Matrix is a methodical way of assessing the business's global marketing and how it may fit into corporate strategy, as shown in Figure 8.

Marketing mix The set of actions, or tactics, that a company uses to promote its brand or product in the market. The 4Ps – price, product, promotion and place – make up a typical marketing mix.

Place The channel, or route, through which goods move from the business selling them to the final user. Place could be the intermediaries, distributors, wholesalers and retailers.

Ansoff's Matrix Suggests that a business's attempts to grow depend on whether it markets new or existing products in new or existing markets. The output from Ansoff's Matrix is a series of suggested growth strategies which sets the direction for the business strategy.

	Existing products	New products
Existing global markets	Market penetration	Product development
New global markets	Market development	Diversification

Figure 8 Ansoff's Matrix in a global market

Exam tip

To score well on any exam question that draws on marketing you will need to use a range of tools such as Ansoff's Matrix to evaluate the issues for a business. A mixed approach may not be appropriate for a specific business, so look carefully at the products it is proposing to sell and the market in which it proposes to sell them.

Ansoff's Matrix may suggest advantages of moving into a global market, including market penetration resulting in greater profitability, and resources of different countries used for producing goods and services possibly resulting in more efficiencies and lower costs. A disadvantage may be that competing in a global market means greater competition and the business may lack resources to compete on such a scale.

Niche markets

A **niche market** is the smaller section of a larger market on which a product or service is focused and is aimed at satisfying specific market needs to create a unique product (covered in Student Guide 1).

Niche market A smaller part of a large market where customers have quite specific needs and wants.

Global niche markets are similar to domestic niche markets in that they target a very specific range of people, though the key is to position a product so that it appeals to a wide range of customers across the global market.

Cultural diversity

Cultural diversity recognises that the ideas, customs and social behaviour of a particular people or society vary in different global markets.

Cultural diversity needs to take into account different values of the market in which the business is operating. For example, in Saudi Arabia not only is the custom not to drink alcohol but it is also illegal to do so. Therefore, Diageo, the multinational global leader in alcoholic beverages, would need to adopt a radical approach to global marketing if it decided to consider the country as a new market.

Cultural diversity means taking into account different interests of potential customers. For example, Adidas needs to recognise that football in the UK and Asia may be big business, but in the US it is seen as a minor sport. In the US, American football would be the focus of Adidas marketing activity for the mass market and football for the niche market.

Features of global niche markets

Features of a global niche market include clear understanding of the wants and needs of the chosen market segment, excellent customer service, expertise in the market, prioritising profit rather than market share, innovation to satisfy changes in markets and cost efficiency that is not at the expense of quality.

Application and adaptation of the marketing mix to suit global niches

For niche markets that are based on luxury and exclusivity, such as performance cars, the marketing mix can be standardised across most global markets. For example, Rolex watches are an expensive luxury Swiss brand that in 2015 had 11.8% of the global watch market. The brand is marketed in the same way across all markets as the typical customer sees the brand as aspirational and appealing to all cultural niches. For example, the car maker Bentley is able to sell its very expensive cars to rich buyers across the globe as the vehicles are seen to be aspirational products that do not have to take into account issues such as local religious beliefs in the way that other products may have to.

To achieve success in non-luxury niche markets, assessment of local customer tastes and behaviour is essential. Tesco started its grocery business in the US convinced that it could adapt to local shopping habits. It failed. Critical factors include distribution, local attitudes and local responses to promotional techniques (in America, they love a coupon).

Cultural/social factors

Cultural diversity needs to consider economic factors such as levels of real disposable income and the traditions of the market, such as religion or lifestyle.

Niche markets need to identify **subcultures** to try to ensure products can take some advantages of economies of scale while appealing to a smaller section of a market across different cultures. For example, even though the culture in Saudi Arabia is different from that of the UK in many ways, a subculture exists that values luxury and exclusive performance cars such as Rolls-Royce and Mercedes.

Subculture Group of people who share a common interest.

With new technologies such as the internet, subcultures are able to communicate more freely internationally and this creates more enthusiasm for these global market niches. For example, when Tesla, the electric car manufacturer, launched its new Model 3 in the US in 2016, global orders went viral. More than 400,000 customers across the world paid large deposits.

Cultural and social factors include the following:
- Cultural differences are how society and customers act in their everyday lives. For example, in India a handshake for a business meeting is considered critical, though Indian women are not supposed to shake hands with men. Any drink such as tea must be accepted as a sign of a willingness to do business.
- Different tastes mean that a business must ensure its product or service reflects local preferences. Primary and secondary market research can help to ensure products meet the needs of the local population. In India, many of the population do not eat meat, so McDonald's has created a unique menu including the Maharaja Mac, a vegetarian burger.

- Although the common business language worldwide is English, there could still be language issues. The business must market its product effectively in the local language and needs access to professional translators and marketing agencies in order to do this successfully. In China, variants of the language are spoken across the country, so different translators are needed to ensure marketing materials are accurate and convey the correct meaning. Unintended meanings need to be avoided at all costs as this will risk damaging the product and brand in the new market.

- Inappropriate/inaccurate translations include the wrong words being used, brand names sounding like something else in the local language, and a brand name being associated with local slang. Even multinational corporations have made mistakes. For example, when Coca-Cola entered the Chinese market, it named its product something that when pronounced sounded like 'Coca-Cola'. The only problem was that the characters used meant 'bite the wax tadpole'. When the company learnt of its blunder, it changed to a set of characters that mean 'happiness in the mouth'. All these issues need careful consideration and appropriate changes should be made.

- Inappropriate branding and promotion create the same issues as inaccurate translations. For example, Colgate, the dental product manufacturer, introduced a toothpaste in France called 'Cue', the name of a notorious pornography magazine.

Knowledge check 16

Give a possible reason why Facebook and PayPal have found it almost impossible to establish a presence in the Chinese market.

Exam tip

Just because a product is niche or desirable does not mean it will be much easier for a business to be successful in a new country or market. You also need to consider ease of access to the market and the social issues unique to each country.

Summary

After studying this topic, you should be able to:
- understand the meaning of global marketing strategy and global localisation and their advantages
- identify and explain the different global marketing approaches
- discuss the application and adaptation of the marketing mix
- identify, explain and apply Ansoff's Matrix to global markets
- identify, explain and apply the marketing mix to a global niche market, including the role of cultures, social factors and subcultures

■ Global industries and companies (multinational corporations)

A **multinational corporation (MNC)** is a business that is based or registered in one country but has outlets/affiliates or does business in other countries.

Globalisation is one of the major reasons for the growth in MNCs. A number of businesses in order to grow and develop have had to take on a global or international perspective. MNCs have also caused further globalisation.

MNCs tend to have their headquarters in western markets such as the UK or the US and other functions such as production in other markets, particularly where there

Multinational corporation (MNC)
A company that has facilities and other assets in at least one country other than its home country. Such companies have offices and/or factories in different countries and usually have a centralised head office where they co-ordinate global management.

is a cost advantage. Table 14 shows the comparative size of the top five MNCs to selected economies to show the amount of potential impact the business can have on a country, particularly emerging economies.

Table 14 Comparative size of top five multinational corporations and selected national economies

Country/Company	2015 GDP/sales ($bn)
UK	2,848
Bulgaria	489
1 Walmart	482
Nigeria	481
2 Sinopec-China	283
3 Petro China	274
4 Shell	264
5 VW	246
Sri Lanka	82
Uruguay	53

Source: Forbes magazine 2015 and World Bank 2015

Given that the income of a company such as Walmart is nearly ten times that of Uruguay, it is reasonable to ask whether multinationals may have too much power over some national governments.

The impact of multinational corporations

Impact on the local economy

Multinational corporations impact local labour, wages, working conditions and job creation. MNCs base themselves in new markets for many reasons, including access to much cheaper labour. For example, the minimum wage for an unskilled worker in Delhi, India, for 2016 was £4.17 per day compared with the UK figure of £6.70 per hour for someone aged 21–24 years. Even taking into account cost of living issues, the benefits to an MNC are clear. So when Burger King moved into India in 2014 it was able to take advantage of cheaper labour costs when pricing its products for the local market. However, the real advantage comes for businesses that manufacture products and then sell them globally as the reduced unit costs can make products more competitive in the global market.

MNCs often pay wages that are higher than local rates and offer better working conditions. Research by the World Bank suggests that MNCs' pay in Hungary and Brazil enjoys a premium over domestic businesses of 6%. This is because the MNCs do not want to be accused of being exploitative. Businesses such as Apple have seen themselves exposed for outsourcing work to China and allowing working conditions to be significantly below a level that fits in with customer expectations of the brand.

Job creation by MNCs can be a large element of the local economy. This can help improve local standards of living. Perhaps more importantly, there is evidence from World Bank research that MNCs bring **skills transfer** to workers and the host country. This helps improve the MNC's productivity and in the longer term the country's skills.

Skills transfer The passing of key skills and technical know-how from an MNC to local workers and the host country.

However, with job creation and increased standards of living over time, local workers' expectations become higher. Trade unions can become more powerful, often bringing safer working practices as well as high pay. This is positive in many ways, but for the MNC the advantages of being based in the country may start to be less apparent.

Table 15 shows the positive and negative impacts of MNCs in this area.

Table 15 The positive and negative impacts of MNCs

	Positive impact of MNCs	Negative impact of MNCs
Local workforce	MNC training methods may improve productivity and employability and lead to skills transfer	May attract over-qualified workforce, denying local businesses of the talents of skilled staff
Wages	Usually pay higher wages than local rates and local businesses, thus improving living standards	Workers without a better job are resentful and local businesses may find a shortage of locally skilled staff to ensure viability
Working conditions	MNCs tend to ensure conditions meet the expectations of western customers so are above the average of the country	Above average may still be regarded as very poor and have a negative impact on the MNC's brand and ultimately sales
Job creation	MNCs have a significant impact on a local economy, which ultimately benefits the country through more taxes being paid and more public services being funded	As MNCs tend to have very efficient cost structures, local businesses may no longer be competitive and jobs could be lost. The issue is whether there has been a net increase in jobs

Local businesses can be affected in negative ways. These include the reduction in the pool of workers available due to the MNC offering better pay and conditions. The size of the MNC may provide significant cost advantages over domestic competitors, making it hard for locals to compete. MNCs bring with them updated technology and more efficient ways of working. 'Technology transfer' occurs when employees learn the new technology and begin relying on it, so they may be unwilling to return to domestic businesses.

Positive impacts include better economic conditions, allowing local businesses to improve their trading position. MNCs often form partnerships with local businesses, perhaps through a joint venture. This means less risk for the local business together with access to new skills and more efficient methods of production. Increased competition acts as a stimulus to local businesses to become more innovative and efficient and may actually uncover local and international markets that a domestic business can use for growth. Skills transfer may occur where MNC workers pass on the knowledge and methods of production they have learnt to local businesses, allowing them to become more competitive.

The issues of local community and environment should be related back to corporate objectives and corporate social responsibility covered in Student Guide 3. MNCs are very aware of the impacts they can have on the environment and local community in which they operate. For example, Kenco, the coffee producer, operates a charitable organisation in Honduras, 'Coffee vs Gangs', which aims to move young people in the local community from criminal gangs to become coffee growers. Not only does this have a positive effect on the local community, it is also a unique selling point (USP) for differentiating the consumer image of the Kenco brand.

With the rise of global pressure groups such as Greenpeace, MNCs are under close scrutiny in terms of how they interact with local communities and the environment.

Knowledge check 17

Why might a business such as Shell Oil be able to sway emerging economies to give preferential terms to oil exploration? What is a potential disadvantage of this to a country such as Nigeria?

From the BP Gulf of Mexico oil disaster in 2010 to issues over drilling for oil and gas using 'fracking', MNCs can show a positive or negative impact on the area in which they operate.

However, there are still numerous examples of MNCs which by mistake or through intention have a negative impact on the community and environment. Some industries such as oil and gas will always carry a level of risk to the environment and local community. In such situations it is often about showing all steps have been taken to minimise the risk in order to reduce stakeholders' negative perceptions. In cases such as that of car manufacturer Volkswagen's seemingly intentional manipulation of diesel emissions tests in 2015, the negative impact on sales and profits can be considerable.

Impact on the national economy

Foreign direct investment flows are the transfer of funds by an MNC to purchase and acquire physical capital, such as factories and machines. For example, the car manufacturers Mercedes and Renault-Nissan announced in 2014 they would invest $1.4bn in a manufacturing facility in Mexico. The benefits to the Mexican economy include 5,700 extra jobs which will boost the local and national economies. This has a multiplier effect on the Mexican economy as not only do these workers have more real disposable income but they and the car manufacturers will pay taxes, leading to improved public facilities such as hospitals and schools.

However, the FDI flow may be positive in the short term but negative in the longer term if the profits made by the new plant avoid Mexico's tax system. Tax avoidance can result in fewer benefits from FDI than had been expected.

The **balance of payments** records all financial transactions made between the country importing goods and other countries. The figures tell us how much is being spent in a country on imported foods and how successful local businesses are in exporting to other countries. For example, in the UK in 2015 the balance of payments was a negative figure of £96.2bn, meaning we imported much more than we exported. In comparison, China's figure for the same period was £654.8bn in surplus, meaning China exported significantly more than it imported.

Deficits tend to cause the value of the currency to go down compared with others, risking inflation. For multinational companies operating particularly in small economies, FDI inflows and outflows can have a significant effect on balance of payments. For example, a large FDI outflow from Kenya, which has a very small GDP compared with the biggest MNCs, would risk pushing down the value of the currency rapidly.

MNCs bring new skills and technology to a country which are then used in the wider economy, such as in other local businesses. For example, in China the US grocery store giant Walmart has transferred not only technology skills related to grocery management but also problem solving and managerial skills to Chinese workers. These skills can then be adopted by domestic businesses. Ultimately this can lead to a better educated and innovative workforce that allows the country to become more competitive in the global market.

Consumers tend to benefit from MNCs as they are introduced to different or lower-cost products with higher quality than local brands. This is particularly true if the

Exam tip

Look at the scale of the multinational in the exam question and compare this to the economy it is entering before considering potential impacts.

MNC has managed to glocalise the product. The main risk to the MNC is through bad publicity as a result of perceptions of reducing local jobs or putting local firms out of business.

An MNC's business culture, which means its accepted norms and values, may be highly professional, with a focus on growth, profit, efficiency and quality. This will benefit an emerging economy as the MNC brings with it a consistent and professional way of working which will ultimately be learnt by domestic businesses. This means an overall uplift in the quality of businesses in the emerging country. However, some MNCs have been shown to operate in unethical ways, with a culture that may bring more harm than good to overseas markets in which they are operating. For example, in December 2010 the British defence giant British Aerospace was fined £28m for bribing officials in Tanzania when trying to get the local government to purchase a military radar system.

Tax paid by MNCs can make a huge difference to any economy but particularly smaller emerging ones. MNCs try to ensure their tax liabilities are kept to a minimum. MNCs with different subsidiaries in different countries find it easy to move profits around the business to those countries where taxation is very low or non-existent. This approach to taxation is called **transfer pricing**, which happens whenever two companies that are part of the same multinational group trade with each other.

When a US-based subsidiary of Coca-Cola, for example, buys something from a French-based subsidiary of Coca-Cola and establishes a price for the transaction, this is transfer pricing. Transfer pricing is managed by MNCs in such a way that the highest profits for the business are in countries which have very low tax levels, such as the British Virgin Islands, where corporation tax is zero. Figure 9 shows the level of corporation tax in various countries in 2016.

> **Exam tip**
> Beware of making it seem as if western-based companies automatically have a purer culture than businesses based elsewhere. Staff in every organisation can be guilty of weaknesses in morality and behaviour.

> **Transfer pricing** Two companies that are part of the same multinational group use internal pricing to artificially transfer profits from high- to low-tax countries.

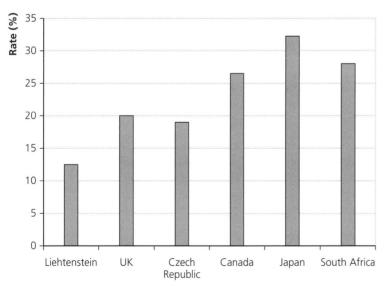

Figure 9 Corporation tax in selected countries, 2016

Source: KPMG.com

Those MNCs using tax avoidance measures to reduce their tax burden have seen a furious reaction from customers and governments. For example, Amazon's UK business made £5.3bn of sales in 2014 but paid only £11.9m in tax. This was tax based on transfer pricing of £679m, with the rest of the £5.3bn sent to Amazon's subsidiary in Luxembourg in order to avoid any tax.

Exam tip

Try to be balanced in your approach to looking at large multinationals and their effects on a country. Try not to stereotype businesses such as oil companies (all bad?) too much as most exist to serve a large base of customers. A well-evaluated answer will draw on key evidence given to you by the examiner together with your wider knowledge to form a balanced judgement of impacts on the market you are asked to consider.

Ethics

Business ethics define acceptable conduct in business dealings and underpin how management should make decisions. Most MNCs have conflicting objectives, such as making profit but at the same time trying to take key moral decisions in the way this is achieved.

This is particularly an issue in economies that have low standards of living, little regulation over what businesses can and cannot do, and a thirst to gain FDI to improve the country's public services. Less developed economies may accept practices that a developed nation may find immoral and illegal, such as allowing very young children to work in factories (just as Britain did in the days when it was a developing economy).

Stakeholder conflicts

A **stakeholder** is a person, group or organisation that has an interest or concern in a business. Stakeholders include shareholders, employees, managers, suppliers, lenders and the community in which the business operates.

For MNCs, stakeholders are more varied and create a complex set of ethical decisions to make in global markets. Shareholder objectives tend to focus on profit maximisation, though another objective for MNCs and shareholders is growth.

Stakeholders such as the suppliers are often in an unequal position of power compared with MNCs, with the risk of MNCs simply ignoring the moral implications of paying very low prices for raw materials. However, some MNCs may have a long-term strategy based on higher ethical standards such as purchasing on the basis of Fairtrade.

Key stakeholders to consider ethical solutions include:

- retailers and suppliers, where price negotiations should avoid bullying smaller suppliers into accepting an unsustainable price
- directors and staff, where there may be huge differences between directors' pay and the minimum wages paid to staff
- management and shareholders, who should beware of the impact of bonuses paid to staff to improve profits based on unethically high-pressure sales techniques

Knowledge check 18

Give one benefit of transfer pricing to shareholders of a multinational corporation. Why do people in the UK believe transfer pricing is bad for their economy?

Business ethics
The study of proper business policies and practices regarding potentially controversial issues, such as corporate governance, insider trading, bribery, discrimination, corporate social responsibility and fiduciary responsibilities.

Stakeholder Group or individual that is affected by and/or has an interest in the operations and objectives of the business. This can include internal stakeholders such as employees and external stakeholders such as suppliers, with different groups having varying amounts of influence over the business.

Pay and working conditions

MNCs operate globally so they have to decide whether it is ethical to have different pay and conditions for staff in different countries. The key issue is to what extent an MNC such as Domino's Pizza should, for example, offer the same pay to subsidiary businesses in the UK, the US and Cambodia, known as a **less economically developed country** (LEDC).

Paying the lowest possible pay to staff in poorer economies such as Cambodia would probably be regarded as unethical, as would allowing very young children to work in Dominos' establishments simply because this practice is widespread in Cambodia. MNCs tend to adopt an approach that can be justified where the rates of pay are greater than the local minimum, thus improving staff's standards of living but still allowing different levels of pay in different local circumstances.

Working conditions also raise ethical issues, including the acceptable and unacceptable examples in Table 16.

Table 16 Working conditions and ethics

Working conditions that could be seen to be ethically acceptable	Working conditions that are unconditionally unacceptable
Cramped and hot where profit margins are too low to allow more space and better ventilation	Dangerous conditions with machinery that is unsafe and the use of chemicals that are known to have serious health hazards
Long working hours of 12 or more hours per day	Forcing people to work long hours by threats or incarceration (which has happened at Apple outsourced factories in China)

Environmental considerations

The key issue here is how far should an MNC go when considering its environmental impact in the area in which it operates? The areas to consider include emissions, deforestation, water and air pollution and waste disposal.

Emissions include those from factories and from the products produced by the MNC. In 2016 Volkswagen was fined $14.7bn by the US government for fixing the diesel emissions on its cars so that they appeared to pass emission standards. Other businesses such as Tesla have made a virtue out of their zero-emissions electric vehicles.

Waste disposal can represent a large cost for MNCs, which may be tempted to put profit before the environment. A report by the United Nations in 2010, which looked at the environmental costs of the world's 3,000 biggest companies, concluded that they would lose one third of their profits if they were forced to pay for loss and damage caused by them to the environment.

Supply chain considerations

The **supply chain** consists of the steps involved in the manufacturing and distribution of goods.

There are many ethical issues MNCs need to consider in terms of manufacturing goods. In less developed countries, labour markets tend to be poorly regulated, which means unethical businesses use **child labour**, which would be regarded as totally unacceptable in their domestic market. The International Labour Organization

Supply chain A network between a company and its suppliers to produce and distribute a specific product. The supply chain represents the steps the company takes to get the product or service to the customer.

estimates there are 170m children working around the world, many making textiles and clothing to satisfy demand in Europe and the US. Places such as Egypt and Bangladesh are some of the biggest areas using child labour. The numbers are falling but clearly MNCs need to think carefully about maintaining an ethical supply chain.

The UK has seen a huge rise in the use of zero-hours contracts. The insecurity implied by contracts of employment with no guaranteed hours gives rise to ethical issues over the distribution of goods. Unions and politicians have campaigned for such contracts to be made illegal, but some businesses only have eyes for the benefit of flexibility to profitability.

Marketing considerations

Misleading product labelling is an ethical issue businesses need to consider. In the US, any cosmetic product that is labelled 'organic' must have at least 70% organic ingredients, that is those grown without chemicals. However, in the UK the rules on organic labelling do not apply to cosmetics. This means, for example, that Boots' cosmetics are legally labelled 'organic' in the UK, even though they contain less than 70% of organic ingredients. In California the labelling would be illegal.

MNCs also can indulge in **inappropriate promotional activities**, such as the McDonald's 'supersize me' approach to selling fast food, where staff were instructed to ask the customer if they wanted to buy a bigger portion than the one they were ordering. Other methods such as 'buy one get one free' (BOGOF) and placing sugary snacks at the checkout in supermarkets are at odds with the current obesity issues in the UK.

Controlling multinational corporations

There is a difference between influencing an MNC, where the aim is to have a positive effect on behaviour, and control, which means restricting the company's actions.

MNCs need to be controlled for many reasons, including the long-lasting effects of mineral extractions, safety standards, the loss of cultures and traditions, and the damaging effects of transfer pricing on the economy.

Political influence

Political influence means that MNCs are often able to exert pressure on government officials, either in the form of lobbying or in some cases having direct connections to those in power. For example, British American Tobacco sponsored a research group which then questioned the government's move to plain packaging only in the UK cigarette market. The government wished to stop any advertising of cigarettes through their packaging, but the research group tried to argue that plain packaging would have no effect in reducing such purchases. Such influence can be seen even more strongly in less developed countries, where cigarette companies hand out free products to young people – to encourage them to start smoking.

Legal control

Governments control MNCs in the way they control any other business: through legislation. From the Trade Descriptions Act to the Health and Safety at Work Act to the more recent Equality Act and Bribery Act, the aim is to ensure MNCs act ethically and fairly without risking the health and wellbeing of stakeholders, particularly workers and consumers.

For MNCs, takeovers and tax are particular areas needing legal control due to the effect the companies can have on the economy, for example in a large multinational buying up a small but popular local brand.

Takeovers become an issue for consideration by the Competition and Markets Authority in the UK where the combined market share of the proposed new company is 25% or more. The government can then decide whether the proposed takeover is in the public interest and block it if necessary. UK competition rules do not apply to MNCs taking over global market shares unless they equate to 25% or more of the UK market.

Pressure groups

Pressure groups can influence MNCs either through direct action, where a physical protest or court action is made to stop an activity, or through indirect action such as boycotting certain types of products. Pressure groups include Greenpeace, Compassion in World Farming and Friends of the Earth.

The pressure group CAAT (Campaign Against Arms Trade) worked hard in 2016 to put a stop to UK firms supplying Saudi Arabia with weapons being used against civilians in neighbouring Yemen. However, in developing economies pressure groups may be seen as applying standards that are unachievable in the current economic situation. For example, China gains the majority of its power from coal regardless of pressure groups viewing this as a pollutant.

It must also be remembered that there are pressure groups that work for MNCs, such as the Confederation of British Industry.

> **Pressure group** A group that tries to influence company policy in the interest of a particular cause.

Social media

Social media has become an increasingly effective tool for individuals and groups to apply pressure on MNCs, as illustrated by Figure 10, which shows the increasing use of the technology.

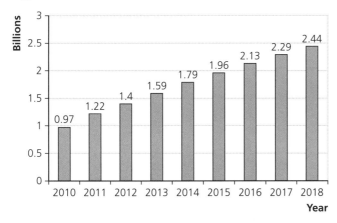

Figure 10 The global rise of social media usage (forecast from 2015)

Source: www.statista.com

As social media allows customers and consumers to spread information freely across a large proportion of the population, and more importantly to an MNC's potential customers, pictures or tweets about unethical behaviour can go viral very quickly. Since MNCs have a high level of public exposure, this also encourages discussion about their behaviour on social media.

For example, the recent Greenpeace 'Save the Arctic' campaign targeted Lego and its partnership with Shell, for drilling for oil in the Arctic. The campaign used a video and Hollywood stars such as Emma Thompson to show why drilling should not take place. The campaign had attracted 5m views and 1.1m hits on Facebook by August 2016.

However, there are plenty of situations where despite social media campaigns MNCs have continued their business activities. In place such as China social media is closely scrutinised by the government so any activities that are deemed to be not in the state's interest will be banned from the internet.

> **Knowledge check 20**
>
> Give a reason why Volkswagen has incurred large fines in the US for lying about the level of pollution its cars produce whereas the UK government has taken no action.

Exam tip

Be realistic about the abilities of different groups, particularly pressure groups and social media, to control or influence multinational corporations. Often people 'care' for a day or two, then forget.

Summary

After studying this topic, you should be able to:
- explain the effects of globalisation on multinational corporations and the effects multinational corporations have on the global economy
- explain and discuss the impact multinational corporations have on local economies
- explain and discuss the impact multinational corporations have on national economies
- explain the meaning of business ethics
- identify, explain and discuss the different stakeholder conflicts a multinational corporation may have to manage

- discuss the impact of the conflicts of pay and working conditions, and environmental, supply chain and marketing considerations a multinational corporation will need to manage in global markets
- explain the political influence a multinational corporation may have on the national economy and the influence social media and pressure groups can have on multinational corporations

Questions & Answers

Exam questions and answers

The questions and answers in this section of the book follow a similar structure to the exams. There are extracts from business situations, data and a selection of all the different types of questions you will be asked to answer in the A-level exam.

Please note that the extracts have been kept to a minimum to allow for a greater range of questions and answers. This means that A-level questions have been related to the same extracts which will not be the case in the actual exams.

All questions give a lower grade answer and an upper grade answer.

Exam structure

A-level Business consists of three two-hour exams. Paper 1 covers half the course: Theme 1 from AS plus Theme 4 from the second year of study (covered in this guide). So the subject content for Paper 1 is Marketing, people and global business. Paper 2, 'Business activities, decisions and strategy', covers the other half of the subject content, namely Themes 2 and 3. Paper 3 covers all subject content, including Theme 1. Each exam consists of Sections A and B, with all questions being compulsory. Sections A and B will have one question broken down into parts based on data and extracts provided in the exam. In Papers 1 and 2 the questions carry 4, 10, 12 or 20 marks. For Paper 3 the questions carry 8, 10, 12 or 20 marks. In the case of Paper 3, the business context for the questions will be issued in the November prior to the exam. Section A questions will be based on the market as a whole (for instance, the UK motor industry) and Section B on a specific company, for example Jaguar Land Rover. The total score for each paper is 100 marks.

Exam skills

For A-Level Business paper 1, questions require knowledge of Themes 1 and 4. Paper 2 requires knowledge of Themes 2 and 3. Questions with 4 marks require knowledge of business terms, specific application of the business term from the extract, and an advantage and/or a disadvantage of the business term related to the extract. These questions may also ask you to calculate answers using formula you have learnt and data in the extract. The examiner will mark this type of question 'from the bottom up'. This means each mark is earned individually so you get marks for an advantage, for example, even though you have not provided any context from the extract. Evidence is anything unique you discuss from the extract in your answer. It must relate back to the question.

Questions with 10, 12 and 20 marks require evaluation of the business term using specific evidence from the extract context. The safest way to do this is to prove a strong, two-sided argument. It also suggests making judgements about the business and the key terms discussed together with proposing solutions to business problems based on the extract and your business knowledge. The examiner will mark these types of question 'from the top down'. This means examiners will give you marks for the highest level of response you show in your answer. A two-sided argument with a good level is required on all evaluation questions, though the level of detail expected will be less than the 10-, 12- or 20-mark questions. It is worth emphasising the statements at the top level (Level 4) of Edexcel's mark schemes.

> 'Accurate and thorough knowledge and understanding, supported throughout by relevant and effective use of the business behaviour/context.
>
> Uses well-developed and logical, coherent chains of reasoning, showing a range of cause and/or effect(s).
>
> Arguments are fully developed.
>
> Quantitative and/or qualitative information is/are used well to support judgements. A full awareness of the validity and significance of competing arguments/factors, leading to balanced comparisons, judgements and an effective conclusion that proposes a solution and/or recommendations.'

Technique when evaluating 20-mark questions

As this is the most challenging answer to write on the paper, the examiner is looking for the evaluation to include some reference to MOPS:

- **Market**: characteristics of the market in which the business operates. How does this influence your conclusion? For example, Apple is in the smartphone market which is dynamic, fast changing and therefore requires a lot money spent on research and development to ensure it keeps its competitive advantage.
- **Objectives**: how do the business's objectives align to the situation in which it finds itself? What are the objectives of the business? How does this influence your conclusion? For example, Apple's objective might be market share, so being the most novel product regardless of the cost may be of greatest importance.
- **Product**: what products or services does the business sell? How might this influence your thinking? For example, Apple may bring out a cheaper iPhone in garish colours to capture more market share.
- **Situation**: what is the current situation the business finds itself in? Does this affect your conclusion? For example, with sales of smartphones peaking, Apple needs to find an extension strategy such as selling to other global markets, for instance India, to maintain/improve market share, hence the need for a cheaper phone.

You need to read the extract and the question and use the most appropriate element of MOPS in this context to help look at the wider issues affecting the business that will influence the key issues in the question.

1 Burger King

Extract A

Incomes in India and the UK in USD: adjusted to show PPP

Country	GDP per capita (2010)	GDP per capita (2015)
India	$4,320	$5,730
UK	$35,900	$38,657

Source: World Bank

Extract B

The fast food market in India is currently worth $12bn, with companies offering local Indian food being the leaders in supplying customers with their favourite dishes. International food chains are smaller players, with only 5% of market share. India has a population of approximately 1.2bn but there are only 2,700 fast food restaurants in the country. In the USA, the home of fast food, the figure is over 50,000.

Fast food restaurants in the USA have reached saturation point, with lots of competition and little growth — for example, there was only 1.1% of growth in 2014. McDonald's dominates the US market with a 47.3% share in 2015, though this is now starting to decline due to increased competition. Competitors such as Burger King have seen their market share drop from 19% to 11.2%. As a result, Burger King has introduced new products and this is starting to pay dividends in increased sales. All fast food businesses are taking great advantage of e-commerce platforms to help with customer orders and choice.

E-commerce in India is fast-growing with sales estimated at $6bn in 2015, a massive increase from the 2014 figure of $3.5bn. This is the largest-growing e-commerce market in the Asia-Pacific area even though it is new and largely untapped. This can be related to the growth in household real disposable income, which in 2015 increased by 10%. Growth in incomes is particularly notable in cities such as Mumbai.

Recent statistics place India as the 130th country out of 189 in terms of doing business, an increase of 4 places since 2015. Starting a business in India is becoming easier, as is access to consistent electricity supplies. Getting permission to construct business premises and paying taxes still remains a problem to business start ups.

Extract C

Burger King is a fast food burger chain based in the USA. It has recently announced that it is looking for an Indian fast food business to help it enter the high-growth fast food market in the country.

In India there is a growing young population with increasing levels of disposable income. The middle class have embraced eating out, partly because of their busy lifestyles, and due to a curiosity to try new types of cuisine. Burger King aims to take advantage of the fledgling Indian fast food market by introducing food that can be ordered in advance, using the growing e-commerce market for goods and services. The company has more than 13,000 restaurants worldwide serving approximately 11 million customers each day in 79 countries. However, its entry into the Indian market is late compared to businesses such as KFC, Pizza Hut, Subway and McDonald's who already have established brands. McDonald's, for example, entered the Indian market nearly 20 years ago.

→

In India most of the population is Hindu, where beef is forbidden. There is also a large Muslim population, where pork products are not allowed. Burger King intends to adapt its product offering to meet these local tastes and practices, just as rival McDonald's has done. It will introduce new options such as the Paneer King Melt, which is a sandwich filled with Indian cottage cheese. In the next few months Burger King plans to open 12 restaurants across India.

Extract D

Jumbo King is a fast food restaurant that is growing across western India. The food often costs less than $1 and includes Mumbai-based dishes such as the vada pav, a potato-based burger in a roll, and to drink, a lassi.

Many of the outlets are based near railway stations, which provides a large number of passing customers — trains are the main form of transport for commuters working in cities. Train journeys often take 2 hours, with 6 million people travelling every day. Jumbo King provides breakfast or dinner on the go for many hungry but time-poor workers. The MD of Jumbo King, Dheeraj Gupta, says the business has been successful as the food is much safer and more hygienic than the many other food stalls that surround stations. The 2 million passengers that travel each day to and from Malad, a Mumbai suburb, prefer their vada pav from a trustworthy provider.

Gupta's next objective is to gain enough funds to expand across India with a new business model. He sees Jumbo King moving to restaurant-style kiosks in order to allow the business to have a more premium appeal and to set it apart from what the local stalls can offer.

GDP per capita (1)

Using the data in Extract A, calculate to two decimal places the percentage change in India's GDP per capita from 2010 to 2015. You are advised to show your working.

(4 marks)

ⓔ The 'calculate' command word means your answer must complete a calculation in at least four stages using data from the extract.

Understanding: this is knowledge of percentage change (AO1) such as the formula for working out a difference between old and new GDP per capita. This is worth 1 mark.

Application: this is for applying the probability formula using the correct figures from Extract A (AO2). This is worth up to 3 marks.

Student A

$$\text{Change} = \frac{\text{Change}}{\text{Original}} \times 100 \text{ ⓐ}$$

$$\frac{5{,}730 - 4{,}320}{4{,}320} = \frac{1{,}410 \text{ ⓑ}}{4{,}320 \text{ ⓒ}} \times 100 = 32.64 \text{ ⓓ}$$

e **3/4 marks awarded** **a** The student uses the correct formula for percentage change and the weighted average, gaining 1 mark. **a, b** They use the correct figures from Extract A to calculate the difference between the 2010 and 2015 GDP per capita to gain 1 mark. **c** The student uses the correct divisor from Extract B to calculate the per capita to gain 1 mark. **d** The student fails to use the percentage sign on what is the correct answer so gains no further mark.

Student B

Percent change = $\dfrac{\text{Change}}{\text{Original}} \times 100$ **a**

$\dfrac{5{,}730 - 4{,}320}{4{,}320} = \dfrac{1{,}410}{4{,}320}$ **b** **c** $\times 100 = 32.64\%$ **d**

---

e **4/4 marks awarded** **a** The student uses the correct formula for percentage change and the weighted average, gaining 1 mark. **a, b** They use the correct figures from Extract A to calculate the difference between the 2010 and 2015 GDP per capita to gain 1 mark. **c** The student uses the correct divisor from Extract B to calculate the per capita to gain 1 mark. **d** The student states the correct answer to two decimal places, gaining 1 mark.

Student A does not follow the instructions in the question closely enough, losing out on 1 mark due to a missed percentage sign – a mistake seen many times under the pressure of the exam hall. Always check your answers for what would have been an easy mark (a B grade). Student B has an excellent understanding of the formula and the calculation and produces the correct percentage change. The student does exactly what the question asks in terms of rounding to two decimal places (an A* grade).

GDP per capita (2)

Using Extract A, explain one reason why GDP per capita may have changed for the Indian economy. (4 marks)

e The 'explain' command word means your answer must include a detailed definition of the keyword or phrase, relate this to the context and give a benefit or drawback appropriate to the question, justifying the point.

Knowledge/understanding: this is for giving a definition of GDP per capita or a reason why GDP per capita may have increased (AO1). This is worth 1 mark.

Application: this is for applying the reasons GDP per capita has changed for the Indian economy using the extracts (AO2). This is worth up to 2 marks.

Analysis/consequence: this is for explaining the benefit of an increasing GDP per capita for the Indian economy (AO3). This is worth 1 mark.

Questions & Answers

> **Student A**
>
> A GDP per capita is a measure of the total output of a country that takes GDP and divides it by the number of people in the country. **a** Looking at GDP per capita particularly over a period of time and in comparison to another economy can be a good indicator of growth. **b** Therefore the Indian economy will become richer and able to afford better standards of living. **c**

ⓔ 1/4 marks awarded a The student gives the definition of GDP per capita for a knowledge mark for 1 AO1 mark. **b** The student then gives a reason why GDP per capita may have changed, but as the answer has already reached the maximum AO1 mark gains no further credit. **c** The student attempts to analyse the benefit of a change in Indian GDP per capita but as the answer is vague gains no marks.

> **Student B**
>
> A GDP per capita is a measure of the total output of a country that takes GDP and divides it by the number of people in the country. **a** According to Extract A between 2010 and 2015 the percentage change in India's GDP per capita has been 32.64%. **b** Therefore the output per person in India has grown, indicating good levels of growth in the country. **c** Therefore this benefits the Indian economy as it is able to raise more taxes and build better schools to create a bigger demand for goods and services. **d**

ⓔ 4/4 marks awarded a The student gives the definition of GDP per capita for a knowledge mark for 1 AO1 mark. **b** The student uses the figures calculated from the first question to point out the percentage in GDP per capita, gaining 1 AO2 mark. **c** They develop the use of the percentage change to highlight that this shows good levels of growth for a further 1 AO2 mark. **d** The student then gives a benefit of a growth in GDP per capita to the Indian economy for 1 AO3 mark.

Student A shows a lack of understanding of the way marks are allocated on this question by giving both a reason and a definition of GDP per capita, even though it is worth only 1 mark. The student fails to appreciate that data from the previous answer and analysis of this can form the basis of two further marks and the attempt at analysis is too weak to gain credit (an E grade). Student B shows clear understanding and skill in writing a concise and well-focused answer for full marks (an A*).

Push factors

Using the data in Extract B, assess the push factors that may have contributed to expansion into India for a business such as Burger King. (10 marks)

ⓔ The 'assess' command word means you need to provide an extract-based answer with advantages and disadvantages of the business concept. The question is asking for benefits of a business having push factors for expansion, with the highest skill evidenced being evaluation. Using Extract B will help provide the evidence for the question and you should refer to it.

Level 1: this is for giving a pull factor or a definition of a push factor. The student will not have used application correctly. There will be no advantages/ disadvantages or they will be poorly discussed. This is worth a maximum of 2 marks, for example by giving an example of a push factor.

Level 2: this is for giving an implication of push factors for the business. The student will have used application correctly. There will be an advantage or a disadvantage. This is worth up to 2 marks.

Level 3: this is for giving a benefit of push factors to the business. The student will have used application correctly. There will be an advantage and a disadvantage which have used application correctly. This is worth up to 2 marks.

Level 4: this is for giving a reason why the push factors may not be useful to the business. The student will have used application correctly. There will be an advantage and a disadvantage which have used application correctly. The advantages and disadvantages will link together and the evaluation will be detailed. This is worth up to 4 marks.

Student A

Push factors are reasons a business may want to grow outside of the domestic country they currently operate in. **a** One push factor on Burger King (BK) may be the high levels of domestic competition in the US market. **b** BK could benefit from entering the Indian market as there is less competition as according to Extract B there are only 2,700 fast-food chains. **c** As a consequence, BK can invest heavily in restaurants and experience rapid growth due to the potential domestic fast-food businesses only having 5% of the market. **d** However, BK are late arrivals to the market and will find well-established competitors such as McDonald's have already gained such a competitive edge over them that growth will be difficult in India. **e**

I think that BK should still expand into the Indian market as there are plenty of opportunities due to there being a growing middle-class population who want to try out new foods. **f**

---

e **3/10 marks awarded** **a, b** The student gives an accurate definition of a push factor with sufficient evidence for Level 1 and 2 marks. **c** The student gives a further benefit of entering the Indian market though this is a pull factor so is not answering the question and gains no marks. **d, e** The points the student makes are an attempt to show a benefit of BK moving into the Indian market but it is not clear whether this is related to a push factor, though use of evidence from the extract is made, so gains only 1 mark and Level 2 (3 in total). **f** The student attempts to draw a conclusion but it is generic and undeveloped so gains no further mark.

Student B

Push factors are reasons a business may want to grow outside of the domestic country they currently operate in. a One push factor on Burger King (BK) may be the saturated US market which only grew by 1.1% in 2014. b BK have lost market share in the US due to fierce competition from McDonald's and now only have 11% of the market and together with the fact that there are 50,000 fast-food outlets BK will be looking to India where there are only 2,700 fast-food outlets to help grow its global business. c As a consequence, BK can invest heavily in restaurants and experience rapid growth in the Indian market, which will tempt young middle-class customers from local independents, thus improving sales revenue. d However, BK are late arrivals to the market and will find well-established competitors such as McDonald's may have already gained a competitive edge over them so that growth will be difficult in India. e BK will also need to invest heavily in new products such as the Paneer King Melt and these costs may offset any gains made in increased global revenue in the short term. f

However, BK may also be looking at the lack of potential growth in the US market compared to the massive potential growth in the Indian market as there are only currently 2,700 fast-food restaurants and a great deal of the 1.5 billion population who have no access to any US chain. g BK operates in 79 countries so clearly has the capacity and financial ability to grow the business in India and it is likely at this stage the biggest threat to growth is from BK's ability to compete against independent fast-food retailers. h Push factors together with a market that is clearly capable of significant growth are an opportunity too good to miss for BK in its global expansion plans. i

e **9/10 marks awarded** a, b The student gives an accurate definition of a push factor with clear evidence of why BK is expanding into India for Level 1 and 2 marks. c The student gives an explanation as to the push factor with plenty of evidence from the extracts, gaining Level 2 and 1 mark (3 in total). d The student gives a benefit of the pull factor on expansion into the Indian market with good use of evidence for 1 mark and Level 2 (4 in total). e, f The student gives a drawback of expansion into the Indian market and develops this point to consider competitors and costs, gaining Level 3 and 2 marks (6 in total). g The student gives a further push factor and evaluates this against the previous factor, giving evidence to support the argument for BK entering the Indian market for Level 4 and 1 mark (7 in total). h, i The student evaluates the push factors in the context of BK's global business, using evidence, and what the challenges may be in the context of the Indian market, finishing with a conclusion, gaining level 4 and 2 marks (9 in total).

Student A makes a common error and misinterprets the question to discuss pull factors and the associated evidence from the extract. The examiner will give a student the benefit of the doubt to a point, hence some credit being awarded for this student's analysis. However, the student attempts only one factor, which is insufficient to access the whole range of marks, and with a weak attempt at a conclusion it is a poor attempt at this question (a U grade). Student B makes a sophisticated attempt to answer this question using a great deal of evidence and looking at the push factors from the US market. There is no need to present a detailed recommendation or conclusion. However, the student needs a little more explanation in evaluation so fails to gain full marks. Nevertheless an excellent overall answer (an A*).

Market attractiveness

Assess the market attractiveness of the Indian fast-food market for a business such as Burger King.

(12 marks)

e The 'assess' command word means you need to provide an extract-based answer with advantages and disadvantages of the business concept. You also need to make a judgement about the business term in the context of the extract and include other relevant business theories. The extracts can be used to provide evidence but the words 'such as' in the question mean you can base your application on any similar business.

Level 1: this is for giving a reason why India may be attractive as a market to Burger King or a definition of market attractiveness. The student will not have used application correctly. There will be no advantages/disadvantages or they will be poorly discussed. This is worth a maximum of 2 marks, for example defining market attractiveness.

Level 2: this is for giving a reason why India may be attractive as a market to Burger King or a definition of market attractiveness. The student will have used application correctly. There will be an advantage or a disadvantage. This is worth up to 2 marks.

Level 3: this is for giving a reason why India may be attractive as a market to Burger King or a definition of market attractiveness. The student will have used application correctly. There will be an advantage and a disadvantage which have used application correctly. This is worth up to 4 marks.

Level 4: this is for giving a reason why India may be attractive as a market to Burger King or a definition of market attractiveness. The student will have used application correctly. There will be an advantage and a disadvantage which have used application correctly. The advantages and disadvantages will link together and the evaluation will be coherent and wide ranging. A judgement will be made about business term in the context of the question. This is worth up to 4 marks.

Student A

One measure of market attractiveness that may be useful to Burger King (BK) is growth in disposable income. **a** Extract B says the level of growth in disposable income in 2015 has been 10%. **b** As a consequence, BK are likely to be able to sell fast food to those people in India who now have more disposable income to spend on luxuries. **c** This will mean BK's expansion into this new market is more likely to generate the revenues and growth the business is hoping to secure. **d**

However, as Extract C states, there is a rush of western fast-food companies entering the Indian market. This means there will be a lot of competition so BK may not be as successful as they hope to be. **e** This means BK will not make the level of sales they may hope for and could end up making a loss. **f**

Another measure of market attractiveness is the infrastructure of India. g As India may have poor roads and electricity supply it may be difficult for BK to set up fast-food restaurants. h This means that BK will not be able to expand into the Indian market quickly and may have to spend more money on initial setup costs, resulting in lower profits and slower growth. i

India is a large market with 1.5 billion people who have a lot more disposable income and few fast-food restaurants, so weighing up the benefits and drawbacks I would recommend that India is an attractive market for BK to enter as they will end up making a lot of profit. j

e **8/12 marks awarded** a The student gives a measure of market attractiveness for 1 mark and Level 1. b–d The student develops the benefit of growing disposable income which is developed using evidence and related back to Burger King, gaining 3 marks and Level 2 (4 in total). e, f The student then gives a drawback of the Indian market with evidence and some development, gaining 2 marks and Level 3 (6 in total). g–i The student develops another measure of market attractiveness and a drawback of this to Burger King, though they do not use specific evidence, and gains 1 mark and Level 3 (7 in total). j The student attempts to make a recommendation using evidence which is not well developed so gains Level 3 and 1 mark (8 in total).

Student B

Market attractiveness is a measure of the potential value of a particular market in a country. a Clearly there is a large growth in disposable income, with Extract B showing in 2015 disposable income grew by 10%. b As a consequence, the young Indian middle class have more money to spend on luxury goods such as fast food. c As BK are clearly trying to grow into an untapped market of currently only 2,700 fast-food chain outlets, the market will be attractive as their investment is more likely to be successful due to Indians having the income to generate sales. d The market is made even more attractive by the fact that Extract B states the market is worth $12bn so could prove a great source of revenue and profit for BK. e However, there already appears to be a significant amount of competition from the local independent food outlets and other foreign brands such as McDonald's. f As BK has little or no local knowledge of the market compared to more well-established competitors, in order to make the market more attractive they will need to spend money on market research to decide where the most profitable locations may be to base their new stores, which means incurring costs, which together with the risks of competition may make the market less attractive. g

Ease of doing business in India, another measure of market attractiveness, does seem to be improving based on some measures such as starting a business. h As India has gone up the World Bank rankings and it is likely to be easier to start up BK's new restaurants compared to McDonald's startup 10 years ago, this is less likely to be a barrier to entry and means that even though research costs may be high, BK can get a return on their investment much more quickly, particularly with a large market of 1.5bn people with increased disposable income. ⌊ This means that India will remain a very attractive potential market, with BK likely to make more than enough revenues back from initial setup costs and market research done to enter the market. ⌋

Perhaps with a fast-growing economy and e-commerce growing at 70% BK may be entering the Indian market at a time when they can offer a blend of localised food, using technology, with better access to infrastructure. This could capitalise on middle-class appetites to eat out and try new foods in a way that other competitors such as McDonald's have not yet managed to do in a big way, meaning the Indian market may be the most attractive it is likely to be to gain the most growth and revenue opportunities for BK. ⓚ

ⓔ **11/12 marks awarded** ⓐ The student gives a definition of market attractiveness for Level 1 and 1 mark. ⓑ-ⓔ A measure of market attractiveness based on growing disposable income is well developed using evidence and related back to Burger King, gaining 4 marks and Level 3 (5 in total). ⓕ, ⓖ The student then gives a drawback of the Indian market, with evidence and development, gaining 2 marks and Level 3 (7 in total). ⓗ-ⓙ The student develops another measure of market attractiveness in detail, with evidence, gaining 2 marks and Level 4 (9 in total). ⓚ The student makes a judgement on market attractiveness for Burger King, with evidence and reference to MOPS, gaining Level 4 and 2 marks (11 in total).

Student A presents a range of measures of attractiveness, with the first one reasonably well developed, but fails to make good use of evidence and chains of reasoning throughout the answer. They make an attempt at a judgement but again it needs more explanation (a B overall). Student B uses two measures of attractiveness, with excellent use of evidence and development throughout the answer. The second measure is not specifically evaluated so even though the judgement and recommendation are well developed and include reference to MOPS, the student just misses out on full marks (though an A* answer still).

Global joint ventures and mergers

Burger King is looking for a local business to help to meet its objective of growth in the Indian market using one of two options, merger or joint venture with Jumbo King (Extract D).

Evaluate these two options and recommend which is the most suitable for a business such as Burger King.

(20 marks)

ⓔ The 'evaluate' command word means you need to review the pros and cons of the business term using case study material. Weigh up strengths and weaknesses of arguments and then support a specific judgement, forming a recommendation and conclusion. You can use Extracts A–D to provide application but the words 'such as' in the question mean you can base your application on any similar business.

Questions & Answers

Level 1: this is for giving a reason, a definition or some knowledge of a merger or joint enterprise. The student will not have used application correctly. There will be no advantages/disadvantages or they will be poorly discussed. This is worth a maximum of 4 marks, for example by giving detailed definitions of joint venture and merger.

Level 2: this is for giving a reason, a definition or some knowledge of a merger or joint venture. The student will have used application correctly. There will be an advantage or a disadvantage of merger and/or joint venture but they will be poorly developed. This is worth up to 4 marks.

Level 3: this is for giving a reason, a definition or some knowledge of a merger or joint venture. The student will have used application correctly. There will be an advantage and a disadvantage which have used application correctly for merger or joint venture. There may be evaluation of merger or joint venture but it is poorly developed. This is worth up to 6 marks.

Level 4: this is for giving a reason, a definition or some knowledge of a merger or joint venture. The student will have used application correctly. There will be an advantage and a disadvantage which have used application correctly for merger or joint venture. The advantages and disadvantages of merger and/or joint venture will link together coherently and the evaluation will be detailed and wide ranging. A judgement and recommendation will be made about the best approach for the business, with a conclusion. This is worth up to 6 marks.

Student A

A global merger is where two separate businesses decide to become one single business, often to save costs and increase market competitiveness. a A benefit of Burger King (BK) merging with Jumbo King (JK) is that it spreads the risk of operating in the Indian market. b As BK are new to the Indian market and JK are well established, BK will gain local expertise in selling fast food. c This means BK is less likely to make poor choices as to what type of food should be on their menu and this will mean lower startup costs and less risk of wasted food and low sales. d However, a merger with JK will require BK buying up the business and forming a new business, which will cost money and may not be something that either party, especially the managing director of JK, wants. e This is because Extract D states JK want money for expansion rather than a multinational company merging with the current operation. f As a consequence, there may be conflict between senior managers of BK and Mr Gupta that leads to clashes of personality and culture which undermines the benefits of a merger and results in a failed merger or one that has more risks than if BK entered the market alone. g

A joint venture is a separate business entity created by two or more parties, involving shared ownership, returns and risks. h BK and JK may find a joint venture is the better approach as the business will form a partnership as the parties will be entering into the business with clearer objectives. i The joint venture will allow BK to still gain knowledge from JK's local expertise and create a more glocalised offering for potential customers, such as restaurants and train station outlets offering a mixture of BK and JK's food. ⓙ However, a joint venture is still likely to have problems such as misunderstandings over the role of each business, leading to the risk of poor decision making and loss of profits and growth. ⓚ

In conclusion, a joint venture may be the best approach for JK as Gupta can keep his own business and benefit from BK's financial input into the new business. ⓵ As a consequence, JK's objective of being able to move into more restaurant-style kiosks will be supported by BK. ⓶ This means the joint venture will be successful due to JK's proven track record with fast food, which means BK will also be successful. ⓷

ⓔ **8/20 marks awarded** ⓐ The student gives a definition of merger for Level 1 and 1 mark. ⓑ–ⓓ The student gives a benefit of merging to Burger King and develops this using evidence but does not relate this back to growth so gains 2 marks and Level 1 (3 in total). ⓮–ⓖ The student develops a drawback of the merger using evidence but this again is not specifically related to the issue of growth for Burger King so gains Level 2 and 3 marks (6 marks in total). ⓱ The student gives a definition of joint venture which is accurate but gains no further marks as Level 1 has already been surpassed. ⓲,⓳ A benefit of joint venture is developed with relevant evidence but does not relate to Burger King's growth objective so gains 1 mark and Level 2 (7 in total). ⓚ The student gives a general problem with joint ventures without evidence but does attempt to link this to the issue of growth, gaining 1 mark and Level 2 (8 in total). ⓵–⓷ The student attempts to make a recommendation with evidence supporting the discussion. However, they misinterpret the question and incorrectly make a judgement for the best approach for Jumbo King rather than Burger King, so they gain no further marks.

Student B

A global merger is where two separate businesses decide to become one single business, often to save costs and increase market competitiveness. ⓐ As Burger King (BK) aim to increase growth, a merger with a local business such as Jumbo King (JK) will not only allow BK to take advantage of an already established network of fast-food outlets at train stations, but take advantage of the local expertise and knowledge Gupta, the managing director, has gained. ⓑ As a consequence, BK will be able to add already successful food ranges such as vada pavs to the Paneer King Melt, potentially gaining very fast growth from the middle-class young train users who may want to try different fast food to what they are used to. ⓒ BK can also introduce this type of food into its more traditional restaurants, perhaps offering a range of products that has a competitive advantage to both other multinational corporations such as McDonald's and local businesses. ⓓ However, a merger normally involves two businesses of a similar size and clearly BK would be the dominant partner, which may cause diseconomies of scale. ⓔ For example, Gupta may be used to being able to make very quick decisions, but in the newly merged business it is likely decisions will take significantly longer, perhaps leading to a loss of the competitive edge gained from the merger and ultimately slower growth for BK. ⓕ

A joint venture is a separate business entity created by two or more parties, involving shared ownership, returns and risks, which may actually be a much better approach for BK and its growth objective. g This is because the joint venture could establish Gupta as an equal partner, which is unlikely to happen in a merger, so allowing BK to benefit from his expertise in the local market while the venture would benefit from the substantial financial resources of the multinational corporation. h BK and JK could find common ground to run the joint venture on as both businesses are clearly keen on growth and BK would gain a USP in terms of its food offerings and unique siting of restaurants and outlets. i For example, it is more likely that Gupta will be able to gain local government approval for BK's restaurants due to his local success, which will ensure growth and ultimately profits will be made quickly. j However, BK may not set realistic objectives for growth for the new joint venture and common goals of both businesses may not align sufficiently to ensure success in terms of the levels of growth returns BK is seeking. k

As BK are a late arrival to the Indian fast-food market they have both local competitors and other multinational competitors such as McDonald's to deal with before achieving their objective of growth. l The key to success in terms of growth for BK is to gain sufficient local expertise to create a differentiated product offering that gives a competitive edge over the two types of competitors. m Merger can only really be a successful method of achieving this with a domestic partner that is of a similar size as it will become a takeover, which risks losing the USP that BK need to achieve growth with. n A joint venture with JK has the greater chance of success as both parties wish to grow. o The key to success is allowing sufficient flexibility for BK to benefit from the local knowledge and tried and tested food offerings while introducing the growing wealthy middle class to a range of fast foods that tempts them away from competitors. p If the terms of a joint venture can achieve this balance, BK should see significant growth in the Indian market. q

e **17/20 marks awarded** a The student gives a definition of merger for Level 1 and 1 mark. b–d The student gives a benefit of merging to Burger King and develops this in detail, using evidence relating this back to Burger King's objective of growth, so gains 4 marks and Level 2 (5 in total). e, f The student develops a drawback of the merger using detailed evidence and relates this back to the growth objective and gains Level 2 and 3 marks (8 marks in total). g–j The student develops the benefits of a joint venture and compares the benefits over a merger. The benefits are related back to Burger King's objective of growth, gaining 4 marks and Level 3 (12 marks in total). k The student gives a drawback in terms of growth of a joint venture, though it lacks development so gains 1 mark and Level 3 (13 in total). l–q The student uses MOPS and evidence to evaluate and recommend the most appropriate approach to achieving the best levels of growth for Burger King. This includes a recommendation as to how this might be achieved, gaining 4 marks and Level 4 (17 in total).

Student A makes the mistake seen regularly by examiners of not answering the question. Instead of evaluating the benefits of the two options in terms of the ability to meet Burger King's growth objective, the student mainly gives the advantages and disadvantages of mergers and joint ventures. Even though they make reasonable use of evidence, the examiner can only give a low mark in this case (an E grade). Student B gives a comprehensive answer which uses a great deal of evidence to evaluate the benefits and drawbacks of a merger and then compares this to a joint venture. The student fails to evaluate a joint venture, and the recommendation and judgement, though comprehensive and using MOPS, are a little repetitious of earlier comments, meaning the student does not achieve full marks (an A grade).

2 The copper industry

Extract A

Antofagasta – costs of mining half a kilo of copper ore in Chile

Component costs	Chilean peso (CLP)
Extraction	1,800
Labour	900
Local permits	100
Transport	100

Extract B

Antofagasta is a Chilean copper mining company listed on the London Stock Exchange and is the ninth biggest in the world. In Chile they own the second biggest mine, Minera Los Pelambres, and employee 19,200 staff. BHP, a competitor, also has mines in Chile, the country producing a third of the world's copper, and is keen to challenge Antofagasta's efficiency of extraction. Copper is sold on the international market and the price fluctuates significantly based on success of the global economy.

Antofagasta produced 400,000 tonnes of copper in 2015, a decrease from 2014's total of 455,000 tonnes. Last July, Antofagasta announced that it would acquire a 50% interest in a rival's copper mine in Chile for roughly $1bn. Antofagasta has decided to tackle the 24% reduction in the price it is getting for copper in 2015 by aggressive cost cutting and investing heavily in automation. While the weaker peso helped to reduce Antofagasta's costs – because it sells in US dollars – the chief executive added that more than a third of its cost-cutting was 'hard cost reduction' arising from 'changes in the way we do things. Most of the changes are structural and we should be able to sustain these going forward'. There was $1.75bn sales revenue in 2015, though profits were down 83% from the previous year.

Antofagasta is also looking actively at pursuing a lower developed country production strategy where extraction costs are significantly reduced, such as Peru. Workers are paid on average 44% less in Peru than Chile and health and safety laws regarding mining are not as strict. Antofagasta is also considering moving its headquarters from Chile to Ireland in order to pay 50% less tax through a system of subsidiaries.

Questions & Answers

Extract C

The top 3,000 multinationals are said to cost £1.4tn per year in pollution and disruption to countries in which they are based or a third of profits. Antofagasta has a mixed track record, with recent claims in its operations in Chile and South Africa that it has ruined local water supplies, built dams that are at risk of collapse and indirectly caused local populations to suffer illnesses, due to the poisons created in the copper mining process entering local rivers. There are also worries in Chile about damage to important archaeological remains.

However, the multinationals have been praised for their wealth creation in local communities, with 21.1m jobs created in the last 10 years, and particularly in the mining industry the huge level of infrastructure brought to emerging economies, including new roads, power supplies and fresh water. Antofagasta has made great efforts to engage the local communities. Anti-poverty group War on Want, which protested at the FTSE 100 copper miners' annual meeting earlier this week, accused Antofagasta of a string of failings.

It cited complaints from locals that the Caimanes community has suffered both contamination and shortages of water due to the presence of the mine. The Chilean government has threatened to levy a large fine equivalent to 10% of Antofagasta's annual sales revenue if action is not taken to resolve the problems.

However, Antofagasta has started to invest much more heavily in environmental and social welfare projects. In 2015 it set up local schools with the government in Chile and has promised $20m towards a new housing project for its mine workers, plus a new hospital for the local community in partnership with the government.

Extract D

The government has invested £50m in state of the art machinery in the Bhubaneswari open cast copper mine in Peru, in order to improve productivity and make the mine the most cost efficient in the world. This includes driverless vehicles that collect and deliver the copper to a refinery, which means the mine can run with 50% fewer staff than competitors require. The mine is currently open to the highest bidder in the mining industry to lease. The Bhubaneswari open cast mine has a capacity of 20m tonnes per annum. Essel Mining, a specialist mining company, are offering staff services needed to bring the mine online. Essel have a proven track record of cutting costs in copper mining, though their fees are quite large and contracts for extraction sometimes lack flexibility.

According to the Peruvian government, two further copper fields are open to extraction, including Kaniha, which needs a significant amount of investment before it can become profitable. The government has offered a subsidy of 25% of the setup costs to any company that agrees a 25-year lease of the mine.

Exchange rates

Antofagasta plc adds a markup of 11.2% to the costs of extraction of copper from its mine in Chile. It then sells the copper on the London metal exchange.

Using the data in Extract A, calculate the selling price of half a kilo of extracted ore, to two decimal places, if the exchange rate is £1 = CLP 1758.84. You are advised to show your working.

(4 marks)

(e) The 'calculate' command word means your answer must complete a calculation of four stages using data from the case study. This can include simple mathematical equations such as percentages and formula you have learnt.

Understanding: this is for working out the total unit cost of the product from Extract A (AO1). This is worth 1 mark for correct calculation.

Application: this is for adding the markup onto the unit costs and working out the UK selling price of half a kilo of extracted ore using the exchange rate (AO2). This is worth up to 3 marks.

Student A

Unit cost extracted copper = 1,800 + 900 + 100 + 100 = CLP 2,900 a

Antofagasta markup price CLP × 11.2% = CLP 324.8 + 2,900 = 3224.8 b

Conversion from Chilean peso price to UK £ = $\dfrac{3224.8}{1758.84}$ c

UK retail price = £1.84 per half kilo d

(e) **3/4 marks awarded** a The student calculates the unit cost of half a kilo of copper, worth 1 knowledge mark. b The markup price is calculated correctly, worth 1 application mark. c The student gives an accurate set of figures for the calculation of Chilean peso to UK price and scores 1 mark. d The student fails to calculate the UK price accurately to the nearest penny so fails to gain this mark.

Student B

UK retail price = £1.83 per half kilo a

(e) **4/4 marks awarded** a The student gives the correct answer to two decimal places so gains the full 4 marks.

Student A makes a mistake that loses 1 mark due to inaccurate rounding of the answer but shows all their workings to gain 3 marks overall (a B grade). This is a typical pressure mistake so make sure you check your calculations carefully. Student B gets 4 marks without any calculations which is allowed by the exam board as it is presumed that to get the correct answer the calculations must have been done separately to the answer booklet. To be safe, always provide workings out (an A*).

Questions & Answers

Specialisation

Explain one reason why specialisation is a benefit to a multinational mining company such as Antofagasta plc. (4 marks)

ⓔ The 'explain' command word means your answer must include a detailed definition of the keyword or phrase, relate this to the context and give a benefit or drawback appropriate to the question, justifying the point. Knowledge/understanding: this is for giving a definition of a specialisation or a reason why specialisation may be a benefit (AO1). This is worth 1 mark.

Application: this is for applying the reasons specialisation is a benefit using the extracts (AO2). This is worth up to 2 marks.

Analysis/consequence: this is for explaining the benefit of specialisation for a business (AO3). This is worth 1 mark.

> **Student A**
>
> Specialisation is when a business concentrates on making one product. **ⓐ** An advantage of specialisation is that it gives a business a competitive advantage over others in the market as it allows higher output in production due to the efficient division of labour. **ⓑ** However, a disadvantage of specialisation is the business lacks a diverse range of skills and products so could be at risk of making huge losses if the market conditions change as there will be no products to fall back on. **ⓒ**

ⓔ 2/4 marks awarded ⓐ The student gives the definition of specialisation for a knowledge mark for 1 AO1 mark. **ⓑ** They then give an advantage of specialisation for 1 AO3 mark. **ⓒ** The student gives a drawback of specialisation but as this is not answering the question gains no marks.

> **Student B**
>
> One benefit of specialisation for Anto is that they are able to benefit from economies of scale to try and minimise costs. **ⓐ** According to the extract, Anto have suffered a 24% reduction in price paid for their copper in 2015, which means the amount of profit they make has significantly reduced. **ⓑ** By being an MNC that specialises in copper mining, costs such as for extracting the copper on a very large scale will be reduced compared to other competitors who have not specialised. **ⓒ** As a consequence, Anto may be able to price its copper cheaper than other producers, helping to sell more, and hopefully makes up for the 24% reduction in price through higher sales volumes. **ⓓ**

ⓔ 4/4 marks awarded ⓐ The student gives a benefit of specialisation for a knowledge mark for 1 AO1 mark. **ⓑ** They use the data in the extract which relates to the next point, gaining 1 AO2 mark. **ⓒ, ⓓ** The student develops the point further to show an advantage over competitors of lower costs, using evidence, and gains 1 AO2 mark and 1 AO3 mark.

Student A shows a lack of understanding of the question as they fail to give any supporting evidence with their answer and offer a drawback, which is not what the question asks for (a D grade). Student B shows clear understanding and skill in writing a well-focused answer for full marks (an A*).

Impact of multinational corporations

Using the data in Extract B, assess the negative impacts a multinational corporation such as Antofagasta can have on the country it operates in. (10 marks)

e The 'assess' command word means you need to provide an extract-based answer with advantages and disadvantages of the business concept. The question is asking for benefits of a business having push factors for expansion, with the highest skill evidenced being evaluation. Using Extract B will help provide the evidence for the question and you should refer to it.

Level 1: this is for giving a negative impact a business can have on the country in which it operates or a definition of a multinational corporation. The student will not have used application correctly. There will be no advantages/disadvantages or they will be poorly discussed. This is worth a maximum of 2 marks, giving an example of a negative impact a business can have on the country it operates in, for instance.

Level 2: this is for giving a negative impact a business can have on the country in which it operates. The student will have used application correctly. There will be an advantage or a disadvantage. This is worth up to 2 marks.

Level 3: this is for giving a negative impact a business can have on the country in which it operates. The student will have used application correctly. There will be an advantage and a disadvantage which have used application correctly. This is worth up to 2 marks.

Level 4: this is for giving a negative impact a business can have on the country in which it operates. The student will have used application correctly. There will be an advantage and a disadvantage which have used application correctly. The advantages and disadvantages will link together and the evaluation will be detailed. This is worth up to 4 marks.

> ### Student A
>
> A multinational corporation (MNC) is a business that is based or registered in one country but has outlets/affiliates or does business in other countries. **a** One negative impact an MNC can have on a country is that they can cause damage to the environment and local community. **b** Antofagasta mining operations in Chile appear to have caused the local people to suffer contaminated water, which could lead to the Chilean government fining the business. **c** As a consequence, this could potentially damage the profits of the business and cause Antofagasta to employ fewer workers. **d** This could mean that there will be less tax going to

the Chilean government and a potential reduction in money that can be spent on public facilities. e However, as Antofagasta is a very large multinational with $1.75bn sales in 2015, the fine would have to be large to cause any problems. f

Another negative impact on the country Antofagasta operates in is that as they have suffered a 24% drop in the price they get for copper they may decide to cut jobs in Chile and this would lead to large unemployment as it is the ninth largest producer in the world. g

e **5/10 marks awarded** a The student gives an accurate definition of a multinational corporation for Level 1 and 1 mark. b They give a negative impact of an MNC, gaining 1 mark (2 in total). c–e The student makes a developed point with weak evidence stating the negative impact on Chile of Antofagasta's fine, gaining Level 2 and 2 marks (4 in total). f The student attempts to evaluate the negative impact but as this is done for the business rather than the country gains no marks as it fails to tackle the question. g The student gives another negative impact with some development and evidence, gaining 1 mark and Level 3 (5 in total).

Student B

One negative impact Antofagasta could have on Chile is the environmental damage mining appears to be causing the region. a According to Extract C, companies such as Antofagasta cause £1.4tn of damage through pollution each year and with the companies' copper operations causing water shortages, clearly this is a cost to the country through workers falling ill and clean-up operations. b As a consequence, not only will the local population be unable to work, reversing some of the 21.1m jobs MNCs have created, but this will also have a knock-on effect on the wealth of Chile. c If many people are unable to work through ill health, they cannot pay taxes and the Chilean government can't put money into education and health. d However, Antofagasta seems to be trying to invest more into the environment of Chile with free healthcare, which may go some way to making up for their environmental damage caused. e This will ensure workers are able to return to work quickly, maintaining their income and the tax the government is able to gain from it. f Also, even though Antofagasta seems to have caused damage to the environment and Chile's local population, it is the ninth biggest producer of copper in the world, with $1.75bn sales in 2015, which means Chile will be able to gain significant taxes to help pay for local services such as hospitals, more than offsetting the negative impacts. g

Another negative impact on Chile may be the fact that Antofagasta has seen a 24% reduction in the price it gets for copper, which may mean the company decides to make workers redundant. h As they employ 19,000 workers in Chile, a large reduction in workforce could have a negative impact on the GDP of the country as production will reduce. i A large reduction will also affect the profitability of local businesses which rely on mine workers as they are unlikely to be able to afford the same standard of living now they have been made redundant. ⓙ However, Antofagasta appear to be spending more money in Chile on mining, with a 50% stake in another mine, and this might offset the loss of jobs as the business appears to be expanding in other areas. ⓚ This means that any redundancy may be small and therefore the effect on the economy will not be sufficient to cause a significant loss in living standards or local business activity. ⓛ

ⓔ **9/10 marks awarded** ⓐ The student gives a negative impact on the country for Level 1 and 2 marks. ⓑ–ⓓ They give a detailed explanation as to the negative impact on Chile, using evidence from the extracts, gaining Level 2 and 2 marks (3 in total). ⓔ–ⓖ The student gives a benefit of the MNC operating in Chile which is well developed and uses evidence to gain 2 marks and Level 3 (5 in total). ⓗ–ⓙ A further negative impact on Chile is developed with evidence, gaining Level 4 and 2 marks (7 in total). ⓚ,ⓛ The student evaluates the wider business activities of Antofagasta in the context of the Chilean economy, giving evidence to support the argument for a more minimal impact than is initially suggested for Level 4 and 2 marks (9 in total).

Student A gives some evaluation of the impact of MNCs on a country but the second part of the answer is confused as the student is evaluating the impact on the business rather than the country (a grade D). Student B makes two well-developed evaluative points using appropriate evidence. There is no need to present a detailed recommendation or conclusion. However, the student needs to give a little more explanation in evaluation on the second impact so fails to gain full marks, but nevertheless, an excellent answer overall (an A*).

Ethics

Assess the possible trade-off between ethical behaviour and profit for a business such as Antofagasta.

(12 marks)

ⓔ The 'assess' command word means you need to provide an extract-based answer with advantages and disadvantages of the business concept. You also need to make a judgement about the business term in the context of the extract and include other relevant business theories. The extracts can be used to provide evidence but the words 'such as' in the question mean you can base your application on any similar business.

Level 1: this is for giving a possible reason for a trade-off between ethics and profitability for Antofagasta or a definition of ethical behaviour. The student will not have used application correctly. There will be no advantages/disadvantages or they will be poorly discussed. This is worth a maximum of 2 marks, for example defining market attractiveness.

Level 2: this is for giving a possible reason for a trade-off between ethics and profitability for Antofagasta or a definition of ethical behaviour. The student will have used application correctly. There will be an advantage or a disadvantage. This is worth up to 2 marks.

Level 3: this is for giving a possible reason for a trade-off between ethics and profitability for Antofagasta or a definition of ethical behaviour. The student will have used application correctly. There will be an advantage and a disadvantage which have used application correctly. This is worth up to 4 marks.

Level 4: this is for giving a possible reason for a trade-off between ethics and profitability for Antofagasta or a definition of ethical behaviour. The student will have used application correctly. There will be an advantage and a disadvantage which have used application correctly. The advantages and disadvantages will link together and the evaluation will be coherent and wide ranging. A judgement will be made about business terms in the context of the question. This is worth up to 4 marks.

Student A

Trade-offs arise where having more of one thing potentially results in having less of another. a Ethical behaviour is the acceptable conduct in all a business's dealing with different stakeholders and how decisions are made. b Profit is the financial return that a business aims to achieve to reflect the risk that they take. c One possible trade-off Antofagasta may need to consider is whether the cost of investing in free healthcare in Chile could be better spent on automating their production process so that unit costs can be reduced. d The $20m used on this scheme may be money that they could put towards new mining equipment. e

Another trade-off is between paying reduced costs in Peru for workers' salaries and higher costs in Chile. f This may be regarded as unethical by shareholders and customers of Antofagasta. g This means that their already very low profits will reduce further due to bad publicity and customers buying copper from another mine. h

Another trade-off is between keeping Antofagasta's headquarters in Chile and moving it to Ireland and paying 50% less tax. i This represents a large saving for the business at a time when there has been a reduction in profits of 83%, which may be liked by shareholders as they may get a bigger dividend. j

For Antofagasta they will need to decide which is the best trade-off for different stakeholders and take this approach. k

---

e **6/12 marks awarded** a–c The student gives a number of accurate definitions of relevant business concepts related to the question for 2 marks and Level 1. d and e The student develops a benefit of a trade-off with evidence, though they do not discuss ethical behaviour so they gain Level 2 and 1 mark (3 in total). f–h The student then gives a further trade-off with evidence and development related back to ethical behaviour, gaining 2 marks and Level 3 (5 in total). i and j The student gives a further trade-off using evidence but does not relate the issue to ethical behaviour so gains 1 mark and Level 3 (6 in total). k The student attempts to make a recommendation but has no explanation or development so gains no further marks.

Student B

One possible trade-off between ethical behaviour and profit for Antofagasta is the potential to cut back on environmental and community projects such as the $20m housing project. [a] This type of approach to helping workers does have the benefit of giving Antofagasta a good reputation but clearly costs a significant amount of money which the corporation needs to spend on new machines to ensure sales revenue expands sufficiently to reverse the reduction in profits of 85%. [b] On the other hand, with a workforce of 19,200, staff morale would clearly decline if they felt this trade-off was not socially acceptable, possibly hitting the productivity levels of the mine and, as a result, possibly costing Antofagasta much more money than that spent on housing. [c]

Another possible trade-off between ethical behaviour and profit is the possibility of moving Antofagasta's headquarters from Chile to Ireland to save 50% tax. [d] This appears to be a method of transfer pricing, where two companies, Antofagasta and the subsidiaries mentioned, would act like a supplier and customer in order to reduce the corporation's tax cost. [e] Shareholders may be very pleased with this type of trade-off as their dividend payments are likely to increase and this could also allow the corporation to have much more retained profit so as to purchase new machinery that increases productivity and reduces unit costs. [f]

However, the government of Chile and Antofagasta's customers may see this as unethical behaviour and the adverse publicity could cause customers to stop purchasing copper and go to another supplier. [g] In the longer term the Chilean government may try and force tax payments from Antofagasta, leaving it with a large tax bill and a poor trade-off. [h]

Antofagasta is already having problems with questionable ethical behaviour in Chile and with a reduction of 24% in the price of copper the corporation will have to weigh up very carefully whether the short-term gains such as more profit turn into significant losses through its unethical behaviour. [i] Certainly the effect on staff morale of cutting investment in the housing project is likely to impact on productivity and has the opposite effect to the short-term cost savings it may bring. [j] As the corporation has other businesses as customers, other trade-offs such as tax bill reduction and moving production to Peru are less likely to have an adverse effect compared to if the company was a high-profile brand selling direct to customers. [k] Trade-offs need to be carefully chosen to ensure the right balance between profits to survive and ethical behaviour to different stakeholders. [l]

🅔 **12/12 marks awarded** ⓐ The student gives a possible trade-off using evidence for Level 1 and 2 marks. ⓑ They develop the trade-off with evidence to highlight its benefit to the corporation for 2 marks and Level 2 (4 in total). ⓒ The student then gives a drawback of the ethical trade-off with evidence and development, gaining 2 marks and Level 3 (6 in total). **d–f** The student develops another trade-off with benefits in detail and with evidence, gaining 2 marks and Level 4 (8 in total). **g, h** The student gives a trade-off in terms of ethical behaviour with development and evidence, gaining Level 4 and 2 marks (10 in total). **i–l** The student uses MOPS to look to make a judgement, recommendation and method of implementation based on trade-offs and ethical behaviours to gain 2 marks and Level 4 (12 in total).

Student A offers a range of trade-offs but fails to evaluate them clearly in the context of ethical behaviour (a D grade). Student B uses a range of trade-offs and clearly relates those trade-offs back to the issue of ethical behaviour. The judgement and recommendation include MOPS and look at the short- and long-term implications of particular trade-offs (an A* answer).

Offshoring and outsourcing

Antofagasta is looking to maximise its profits by closing down a mine in Chile and using one of two options, outsourcing or offshoring mining production to Peru (Extract D).

Evaluate these two options and recommend which is the most suitable for a business such as Antofagasta.

(20 marks)

🅔 The 'evaluate' command word means you need to review the pros and cons of the business term using case study material. Weigh up strengths and weaknesses of arguments and then support a specific judgement, forming a recommendation and conclusion. Extracts A–D can be used to provide application but the words 'such as' in the question mean you can base your application on any similar business.

Level 1: this is for giving a reason, a definition or some knowledge of outsourcing or offshoring. The student will not have used application correctly. There will be no advantages/disadvantages or they will be poorly discussed. This is worth a maximum of 4 marks, for example by giving detailed definitions of outsourcing and offshoring.

Level 2: this is for giving a reason, a definition or some knowledge of outsourcing or offshoring. The student will have used application correctly. There will be an advantage or a disadvantage of offshoring and/or outsourcing but they will be poorly developed. This is worth up to 4 marks.

Level 3: this is for giving a reason, a definition or some knowledge of outsourcing or offshoring. The student will have used application correctly. There will be an advantage and a disadvantage which have used application correctly for offshoring or outsourcing. There may be evaluation of offshoring or outsourcing but it is poorly developed. This is worth up to 6 marks.

Level 4: this is for giving a reason, a definition or some knowledge of outsourcing or offshoring. The student will have used application correctly. There will be an advantage and a disadvantage which have used application correctly for outsourcing or offshoring. The advantages and disadvantages of offshoring and/ or outsourcing will link together coherently and the evaluation will be detailed and wide ranging. A judgement and recommendation will be made about the best approach for the business, with a conclusion. This is worth up to 6 marks.

Student A

Outsourcing means a business gets another business to do the work for them, in either the same or a different country. a A benefit to outsourcing Antofagasta's (AF) mining operations to Peru would be that the business could benefit from Essel's proven track record of cutting costs. b As AF has suffered a 24% reduction in the amount they receive for copper, they will need to look for other ways of making a profit. c Extract B says they are looking to move into other markets and this way they could not only do that but get Essel to run the mine for them. d However, outsourcing means that AF will not be able to control the production of copper at the mine in the same way as if they owned it. e This is because Essel and AF will have to make an agreement as to how much copper is extracted from the mine and AF may want a lot of flexibility so as to cope with demand for the material. f

Offshoring means a business getting work done in a different country. g A benefit of offshoring to AF is that they can take advantage of lower costs of production. h In Peru the workers receive less pay per hour than those in Chile. i This means AF can save money on the costs of labour as they can employ less staff at their Los Pelambres mine and move production to the Kaniha in Peru. j This could make a 44% cut in costs as workers are paid this much less than staff in Chile. k However, Extract D states that the Kaniha copper field needs a significant investment of money before it can make a profit. l As AF is trying to cut costs this may put them off from offshoring to this mine. m

AF need to decide whether they want to start production of a new mine in Peru immediately, in which case outsourcing to Essel seems to be the best approach. n If they can wait and invest money in the Kaniha mine they can take advantage of having full control of the mine and of the entire operation. As AF made a massive loss in 2015 the best choice is to outsource. o

---

🅔 **11/20 marks awarded** a The student gives a definition of outsourcing for Level 1 and 1 mark. b–d They give a benefit of outsourcing to Antofagasta and develop this using evidence, with some link back to profits, so they gain 3 marks and Level 1 (4 in total). e, f The student develops a drawback of the outsourcing using evidence but this does not relate back to profits and is a weak explanation so gains Level 2 and 2 marks (6 marks in total). g, h The student gives a definition of offshoring which is accurate but gains no further marks as Level 1 has already been surpassed. i–k A benefit of offshoring is developed with relevant evidence but does not relate to Antofagasta's maximisation of profits so gains 2 marks and Level 3 (8 in total). l, m The student gives a drawback of offshoring to the Kaniha mine, though it lacks some development, so gains 1 mark and Level 3 (9 in total).

n, o The student attempts to make a recommendation with evidence supporting the discussion, with some reference to profit maximisation. As it lacks detailed development it gains only 2 marks and Level 3 (11 in total).

Student B

A benefit of outsourcing to Antofagasta (AF) is that they can take advantage of both the new technology that has been invested in the Bhubaneswari mine of £50m and also the expertise of Essel mining. **a** Looking at Extract B, even though AF are the ninth largest mining company their profits in 2015 dropped massively by 83%. **b** As consequence, just opening new mines alone under their own control may not be enough to turn round this situation. **c** By hiring in the expertise of Essel they can take advantage of more mechanised production in Peru, which should help to cut costs and maximise their profits. **d** However, outsourcing would mean AF would have to pay the large fees of Essel and agree to an extraction contract that will not allow flexibility for supply of copper. **e** This may mean that they will have to get Essel to extract 20m tons of copper per annum from the Bhubaneswari mine but may not be able to sell this at the best price. **f** If copper is not required by the global economy then they will have large costs, excess stock and profit maximisation will not be possible. **g** This could ultimately lead to an even worse drop in profits than those of 83% suffered in 2015. **h**

Offshoring, on the other hand, would not suffer from some of the disadvantages of outsourcing as AF would keep total control of their operations in Peru so would be able to only produce sufficient copper for the demand of the current global market. **i** The extraction costs are significantly reduced in Peru so AF could buy a copper field such as Kaniha and use local staff and its own expertise and equipment to run the mine. **j** If they reduced the number of staff in Chile they could take advantage of the 44% reduction in wages for copper extraction, which would help them maximise profits on all copper produced by being able to sell at a lower price than competitors. **k** The Peruvian government is also offering subsidies on this mine of 25%, which also allows for further profit maximisation by passing this on as a price reduction to customers. **l** However, offshoring has significantly more risks than outsourcing as the Bhubaneswari mine is already up and running whereas the Kaniha mine will need significant investment before it becomes profitable. **m** Offshoring may therefore end up costing AF more in the short term so this would reduce the ability of the business to profit maximise in this period of time. **n**

Clearly a move of extraction to Peru will help AF reduce costs and achieve prices for copper that are more competitive, leading to profit maximisation. **o** The issue is whether AF feels they can wait for the Kaniha mine to be ready for extraction, so as to keep control of the whole operation and be able to better control production to meet demand, or whether they feel the productivity and significant cost gains of the Bhubaneswari mine is the better approach. **p** The trade-off is speed of getting to market with less control over production compared to slow getting to market but more control over production. **q** AF will need to consider these choices carefully, perhaps using investment appraisal techniques, before making a choice, in order to reduce risk and maximise profits. **r**

ⓔ 17/20 marks awarded 🄰 The student gives a benefit of outsourcing to Antofagasta, with evidence, for Level 1 and 2 marks. **b–d** They develop the benefit of outsourcing in detail using evidence and relating this back to profit maximisation, so they gain 4 marks and Level 2 (6 in total). **e–h** The student develops a drawback of the outsourcing using detailed evidence and relates this back to profit maximisation, gaining Level 3 and 3 marks (9 marks in total). **i–l** The student develops the benefits of offshoring for AF and relates this back to maximising profits, gaining 3 marks and Level 3 (12 marks in total).

m, n A drawback of offshoring is developed in detail with evidence for 2 marks and Level 3 (14 in total). **o–r** The student uses MOPS and evidence to evaluate and recommend the most appropriate approach to achieving the best levels of profit maximisation. This includes a recommendation as to how the trade-off could be assessed, gaining 3 marks and Level 4 (17 in total).

Student A's answer adopts a reasonable structure but lacks detailed development of points and is sometimes vague when relating these back to profit maximisation (a C grade). Student B gives a comprehensive answer which uses a great deal of evidence to evaluate the benefits and drawbacks of outsourcing and offshoring. Comparisons are insightful, with a judgement and recommendation made, drawing on other business concepts. With a small amount of further development for the conclusion full marks could have been achieved, but an excellent answer overall (an A* grade).

Knowledge check answers

Knowledge check answers

1 a) With the growth of GDP comes a rise in standards of living and western economies such as the UK have seen a corresponding growth in wage rates. This means that lower economically developed economies such as China with lower standards of living can outcompete UK-based companies on costs of manufacturing products. b) By moving into the services sector, such as banking.

2 A product that has been altered by a UK manufacturer for global sales is the Nissan Qashqai, which is sold with left-hand drive for markets such as the US. The car has been an outstanding success, with 85% being sold overseas.

3 Emerging economies often start with low-level industrialisation and farming as their only products, so in order to industrialise and offer globally competitive products the working population needs to be educated to be able to undertake more sophisticated tasks, such as operating machinery. This requires basic education such as literacy.

4 As the pound fell sharply in its value against other currencies, exporters such as Nissan UK were able to compete more effectively globally as importers could buy more of the UK products for their local currency. Manufacturers that can obtain most of their raw materials from the UK, such as Nissan UK sourcing steel for cars from the UK, benefit the most from the depreciation of the pound, but those manufacturers that have to buy raw materials from abroad will see those costs go up, so they may not get the full benefit of the exchange reduction.

5 Companies such as Apple not only bring investment to countries like Ireland but they bring jobs in associated businesses, such as workers who build the factories and offices. Such a move will also encourage other MNCs to be based there – very good advertising for the nation.

6 As Chinese steel is so much cheaper than UK steel, due to significantly lower labour and energy costs, it would be unprofitable for UK steel plants to sell their product on the global market. Tata could move more steel production to an economy such as India with lower costs so that its steel business would become more globally competitive.

7 One disadvantage of imposing a tariff wall for countries within the bloc can be businesses that are less efficient. For example, a tariff wall on farming products may mean farmers within the protected countries are less pressured to become efficient in the way they farm and produce products. They may therefore become inefficient compared with farmers in other countries such as the US and Canada who have had to adopt innovative technology and the economies of scale to ensure their products are globally competitive. When a tariff wall is then brought down, domestic farmers will have little chance of competing with importers.

8 Emerging economies may have poor infrastructure and industries that are poorly developed compared with global competitors in the West. Forming a trade bloc means resources can be pooled, the trade bloc is more likely to secure better deals with stronger nations, and within the bloc trade is more likely to be fairer as the countries are at the same stage of development.

9 Trade blocs such as the EU offer advantageous trade deals to members, such as free movement of goods which is not offered to countries outside the bloc. It could be said that this promotes protectionism, with those countries outside the bloc having to pay tariffs, artificially restricting free trade globally.

10 In the service sector, for example, there has been a backlash among some customers when companies have outsourced their call centres. The feeling has been that the levels of customer service have been degraded by movement to an emerging economy. So while multinationals may have made savings on wage rates, these are not sufficient to cover the costs of poor customer service.

11 There has been a huge growth in the disposable incomes of the middle classes in China who see certain products such as luxury cars as a sign of success. There are also no equivalent luxury vehicle manufacturers in China so market growth has been free from this type of competition.

12 Costs such as skilled labour are much cheaper than in the US and as NAFTA brings free movement of goods, the cars produced can be sold cheaper and free of tariffs in the US market. Mercedes has offshored production to Mexico for the same reasons.

13 Emerging economies force multinationals into joint ventures so that infant industries are not outcompeted and there are transfers of knowledge between the two partners that can benefit the economy as a whole. The local partner will be able to learn from the multinational in terms of skills and will be protected from outside competition.

14 Aldi achieves cost leadership by keeping the range of products stocked to a minimum so as to take advantage of bulk buying and other economies of scale. Tesco could try to compete on costs but this is likely to take some time. Alternatively, Tesco could compete by differentiating products other than by price. For example, it could offer locally sourced meats and poultry in contrast to Aldi sourcing across Europe.

15 As Chanel handbags are an example of a niche product, the brand has transnational appeal, allowing the business to adopt the same marketing strategy across most markets, thus saving costs on promotional materials and campaigns. McDonald's has tried the ethnocentric approach but found in a number of global markets it was unsuccessful due to different local tastes and cultures.

16 As China is a communist state it has much greater controls over freedom of expression for citizens on the internet. Therefore, Facebook has not been able to enter the Chinese market as it was unwilling to allow the state access to all personal accounts. PayPal is operating in China but as the market was not opened until recently, it has become dominated by the local equivalent Alipay, which Chinese society finds more centred on its cultural requirements. Therefore, PayPal has struggled to adapt and promote its services in this market.

17 Shell Oil is so large that many small countries such as Nigeria are desperate to gain FDI from it. This means they may not get as good a deal from multinational companies compared with western nations, which have much stronger economies. A disadvantage is that Nigeria may turn a blind eye to low pay and poor working conditions for staff.

18 The multinational corporation will be able to significantly reduce its corporation tax bill, leaving more profit to pay as dividends. Countries such as the UK believe transfer pricing is bad for the economy as the multinational corporation is seen as benefiting from consumer purchases in the market but not paying for the infrastructure and other costs that taxes help to pay for.

19 The cost savings can give the business a huge competitive advantage over other businesses in the global market, so it is seen as a worthwhile trade-off. Ethical behaviour can be seen as a longer-term profit making strategy for multinationals based on the positive impact such behaviour has on customers and the fact that there are many instances where the short-term profit made by unethical actions has been more than offset by punitive fines made by governments when the behaviour has been exposed.

20 VW was fined $2.7bn by the US government in July 2016 as the law states that such deceptions attract a fine per car that has been sold – approximately 475,000 vehicles. The UK has not fined VW so far, one of the main reasons being that as part of the EU it is for the trade bloc to take action rather than the UK. As VW is a German company the issue is being treated more carefully as EU jobs may be affected significantly.

Index

Note: **bold** page numbers indicate key term definitions.

Index